The Innovator's Playbook: A blueprint for business breakthroughs

ICO
InnovationCoaching.org

The Innovator's Playbook: A blueprint for business breakthroughs

A comprehensive guide to organizational innovation, providing practical strategies and simple practices to build innovation capabilities that can be used to design, transform and scale radically better ways of working.

Paul C. Wilson
ICO
www.InnovationCoaching.org

Copyright © 2023 Paul C. Wilson

All rights reserved

ISBN: 9798397056502

www.InnovationCoaching.org

For Clay Christensen, who inspired me on a seven year journey, to develop a radically simple solution to the innovator's dilemma

For my son

For problem solvers everywhere

Preface

"The value of an idea lies in the using of it."
Thomas Edison

Many of us have ideas that we believe could change the world, but few of us actually succeed in doing so. The likes of Jobs, Musk, Zuckerberg, and Bezos didn't achieve success just because they had an idea - they found a problem that needed fixing and built businesses that radically improved how we do things. They all followed a similar journey of defining the problem, designing a solution, transforming it into reality, and then scaling it. Imagine if every project team or department had the same attitude and approach towards problem-solving.

Shouldn't we be listening to what problems our employees want to solve? What if there are radically better ways of working just waiting for the right attitude and approach? How much value could they add to the bottom line? As business leaders, don't we have a duty of care to inspire these problem solvers, to incentivize, train, and coach them?

Shouldn't there be a policy giving them permission and the tools to implement radically better ways of working? If only we inspired and taught our employees to find and implement them.

Silicon Valley businesses don't accept dumb ways of working. On the contrary, they expect employees to work smarter and to continuously design, transform, and scale radically better ways of working. Silicon Valley founders lead human innovation platforms inspired by purpose and vision to deliver services and products that solve the world's problems. When these human innovation platforms are super-focussed on delivering solutions, they organically re-organize around the parts of the business that need to work better. There's always a radically better way to work. They continuously use experience feedback from their customers and employees regarding how they experience the products, services, and brand.

This book is based on the observations of Google, Tesla, Facebook, Apple, and many others, living in Silicon Valley running startups. It's a place where you have to decode the human innovation platforms around you and how they create value before you can succeed yourself.

I'm thrilled to present this book, which I hope will immerse you in Silicon Valley and give you a taste of what it's like being there as an innovator. Additionally, I hope it provides insight into the value of human innovation platforms. Perhaps this book will inspire you to build a human innovation platform within your business or to build one as a foundation to solve a significant problem, like achieving net-zero.

There are human innovation platforms everywhere in the world, just waiting for someone with the vision to find a problem worth solving and lead the journey to design, transform, and scale a solution.

If that person is you, I would love to hear what you're working on.

Looking forward,
Paul Wilson

5 June, 2023

Paul@InnovationCoach.org

Contents

The Future of Work and the Need for Organizational Innovation	1
The Organizational Innovation Approach	5
Leveraging Connected Human Consciousness to Innovate	9
The Success Journey of Silicon Valley	13
Bootstrapping for Success	19
You Can Change The World	23
Strategizing for Success in Organizational Innovation	27
Financial Feasibility	33
The Investor's Perspective	39
DESIGN	43
TRANSFORM	47
SCALE	51
Making It Happen	55
Silicon Valley Mentors	59
Silicon Valley Heroes	71
Silicon Valley Investors	81
Your Success Journey	87
Introducing the OI Management Principles	91
A Silicon Valley Mindset	97
Aesop Had the Right Idea	103
Coaching Organizational Innovation	105
Leading a Human Innovation Platform	109
The Significance of Leadership in Driving Innovation	113
The Importance of Human Psyche in Organizational Innovation	117
The Role of Managers in Modern Organizations	123
Organizational Innovation and Corporate Culture	127
OI and Corporate Governance	129

The Importance of the OI Schedule in Prioritizing Innovations	131
OI Principles for Successful Transformation	133
Principle 1: Coaching OI	137
Principle 2: Success Journeys	141
Principle 3: DESIGN	145
Principle 4: TRANSFORM	149
Principle 5: SCALE	153
The OI Desired State	161
The Importance of OI Policies and Charters	165
Designing Organizational Innovation Capabilities	169
Transforming to an OI Active Organization	173
Scaling OI in Your Organization	179
Activating the Human Innovation Platform	183
ICO Global Leadership Team	186
ICO As a Startup	189
Coaching OI As A Service	191
About the Author	194

Part One

Introduction

1

THE FUTURE OF WORK AND THE NEED FOR ORGANIZATIONAL INNOVATION

It's no secret that technological advancements are automating jobs at an alarming rate. How often do you wonder if your job will still exist in the next 5 years? Are you concerned about how long you will remain economically useful?

If you're asking yourself these questions, you're not alone. It's time to reframe how we think about work and the methods we use to do our jobs. This book offers a way to meet the future head-on and help employees, managers, and consultants learn how to contribute to an organization's future in ways that drive radical growth. If you're a consultant, you can bring innovation value to your clients in a structured and coachable way using Organizational Innovation (OI) to develop your client's OI capabilities.

It's better to be co-creating the future than being sidelined by it.

The life-spans of most organizations are rapidly decreasing because they are led by good executives who do their best to avoid organizational disruption, thus losing the opportunity to radically improve. Christensen maintains that they run great businesses into the ground. The same good executives might also run their employees into the ground. Employees in most parts of the world appear to lack innovation awareness and fail to keep themselves up with the times, believing it is not their job to innovate and that they will be up-skilled as needs be, by their employer. They also believe it is some other department's job to do innovation. This is the problem we need to address. Regular employees, when inspired, coached and encouraged to uncover opportunities for radically better ways of working, can create incredible innovations. In Silicon Valley, we observed a common business culture that expects all employees to find radical improvement opportunities in the ways they work. The idea of a human innovation platform starts with adopting and adapting a mindset prevalent in Silicon Valley culture. This innovative mindset prioritizes empathy, digging deeper into the needs of people. Turning these needs into data, then using analysis and engineering to create solutions the world needs, is what makes Silicon Valley such an incredible place to learn from. Organizational Innovation (OI) is about having employees see themselves as innovators, no matter what their job is. An Accounts Payable clerk can undoubtedly improve their process. If only they had a collaborative, multi-faceted team who would listen and a manager who could coach them in OI. A corporate OI policy would encourage and support them, creating the right mindset.

This book can help you find answers and build capabilities to be resilient to the coming changes and find opportunities to thrive. We encourage readers who work in organizations to understand OI and to implement the concepts from Silicon Valley into office and life situations, creating an innovation network around you, in your organization and community, that works in the same way; continuously radically improving.

It's time to take front-end tech-related innovation decisions away from the IT department and give the ownership of work innovations enabled by technology to employees.

In conclusion, the future success of employees, managers, and consultants will focus on how well they design, transform, and scale innovations, beginning with thorough problem articulation. Everything they used to do, will be automated. OI Coaches teach and support coal-face employees, people doing the actual work, to become OI

Innovators, supporting them to design, transform, and scale radical improvements in organizations. Managers are well-positioned to be these OI Coaches.

Understanding OI can help you with a practical approach to developing a human innovation platform that can transform your organization to work brilliantly across the value-chain and better respond to the needs of your employees and market. Get this right, and you will have a new skill that can be valuable in any team, department, and organization.

Across the organization, OI could mean the difference between barely surviving a few more years and radically disrupting your market, ensuring future success in the brave new world of Generative AI and the rapidly developing next generation of AI technologies.

2

THE ORGANIZATIONAL INNOVATION APPROACH

In the ever-evolving world of business, it's important to look for innovative ways to stay ahead. As someone who has founded four cloud software startups in Silicon Valley, I have learned valuable lessons along the way. In this book, I want to share those experiences with you and show you how to apply them in an enterprise context.

Organizational Innovation, or OI, is a business approach that we have developed based on our observations of successful Silicon Valley companies. This approach can be used by businesses, startups, government organizations, communities, and non-profits to develop radical new ways of working.

At its core, OI is a bridge between what is familiar and what is new. It integrates innovation activities using a value-chain composed of DESIGN, TRANSFORM, and SCALE innovation activities to deliver radical new ways of working.

By following this approach, you increase the probability that this 'innovation bridge' to the new is actually useful to employees.

Innovation is not just about implementing new systems or processes. It's about understanding the Success Journey of the Employee. By identifying what bridges they need to cross to a new way of doing things, you can provide an essential part of their Success Journey and, if successful, the Success Journeys of many other employees.

Unfortunately, many startups and business innovation projects fail because people don't understand the Success Journey principles. Instead, they 'misapply' doctrines that are well known all over the world. That's why it's important to use the OI approach, which enables transformations driven by employee-led innovation.

At our non-profit initiative, we work with a global network of OI specialists to set standards and develop global capabilities.

Our goal is to help people and organizations take the lessons from Silicon Valley and incorporate them wherever they may be.

By coaching OI, you can lead this new field with us. It's time to be more prudent in using doctrines like Project Management and the Agile Framework. Let's work together to develop and mature this field of OI.

3

LEVERAGING CONNECTED HUMAN CONSCIOUSNESS TO INNOVATE

In today's world, scalable narrow artificial intelligence (AI) is becoming more prevalent in fulfilling specific job roles previously performed by humans. Although Generative AI is a powerful tool, automating system processes and procedures is where the real enterprise value is at this stage. However, what sets humans apart, for the time being, is our connected human consciousness. Human connected consciousness is the way we choose to be experienced in life by others. While AI is developed to fulfill only its function, we have the ability to transcend beyond our natural intentions.

If we maintain a self-serving level of consciousness, acting out of fear and greed, AI will become our masters, leveraging people with low-level consciousness because it makes them vulnerable to manipulation. This means that marketers' AI can know us better than we know ourselves based on our social media and internet activities. However, if we leverage our value differentiator, our connected human consciousness, we can innovate in a way that AI cannot.

Using connected human consciousness in the Success Journey approach is an effective way to innovate. It involves understanding employee needs and removing the ego from coaching engagements. By transcending our ego and operating from a level of consciousness conducive to relational chemistry, we can truly coach and embrace Organizational Innovation (OI). Empathy is key in understanding the context of employee needs, developing empathic intuition, and moving towards higher connected human consciousness.

As we listen with empathy and dig deeper, we gain a useful understanding of people's real situations. Opportunities to develop and practice empathy arise in our interactions with others, allowing us to evolve our levels of connected human consciousness. OI As a professional philosophy can support our personal Success Journey, bringing greater meaning to the workplace, as our natural intention is to solve people's problems. By using OI to support others, we can be happy and more successful, financially and otherwise.

In Part Two, we will examine Silicon Valley's origin story of Organizational Innovation.

In my opinion, the only meaningful way forward is to leverage our connected human consciousness to design, transform and scale a better reality for humanity.

4

THE SUCCESS JOURNEY OF SILICON VALLEY

Silicon Valley has become synonymous with success, but what is it that sets these iconic companies apart? The answer lies in their focus on helping people be successful at something, rather than simply having an idea and going with it. This approach involves strategy and empathy, and it's what we call "The Success Journey of the Employee."

Steve Jobs visits his childhood home - Photo: CNN

Through years of research and observation, we have developed a method of working based on the common steps followed by successful Silicon Valley companies, which we call the OI Value Chain. This approach starts with understanding what employees need to succeed in their jobs and careers, and it results in large amounts of valuable information and usable data from thousands of employees.

To manage all of this information across an organization, we have built an OI Platform we call 'icntr' It serves as an integrated cloud database for OI Value Chain workflows, business-case modeling, and data-capturing. It's essentially an OI 'System of Records', starting with information from Success Journey discussions around the organization.

The key to success with this approach is to focus on the employee's success, rather than business success. Silicon Valley heroes, such as Steve Jobs and Elon Musk, have shown that building products that solve other people's 'at scale' problems is the key to success. Other people's problems are essential in fulfilling your Success Journey, and you have to make it about their needs, where you can help them, not the great idea you have or the great new app you built or how ambitious you are. The market only cares about how you will help them with their Success Journey.

This approach offers IT departments a better way to create apps that colleagues want to use. By focusing on the employee's needs to make the organization work better, we can create a total environment that responds to what employees need, to do great work.

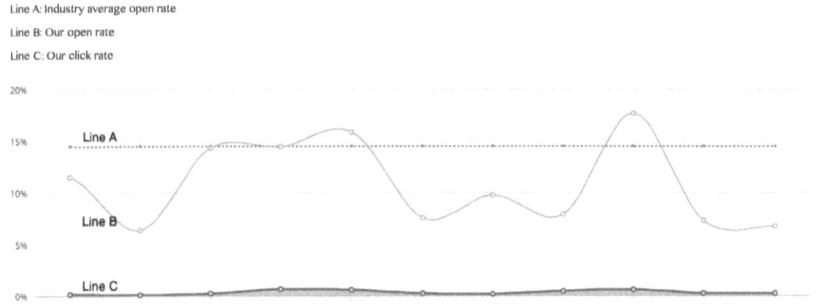

Graph Showing Email 'Open & Click' Statistics Introducing People to Our App

The importance of messaging that reflects the needs of your market cannot be overstated. Our own data can be used to explain this with numbers, represented in the chart above. It's a snapshot across 11 email campaigns sent to 14,000 people over three months. When the subject line of an email addressed the recipient's needs, the number of emails opened exceeded the industry average. Additionally, the introduction of an app that solved people's innovation and transformation problems resulted in a 4.6 times increase in interest to read an email.

This data clearly shows that messaging must be focused on solving the specific problems of your market in order to be effective.

It's important to note that simply touting the features of your product or service, without addressing the needs of your market, will likely not lead to success. The market only responds to messaging that is clear about how it will help them solve their particular problem. This may require a shift in thinking for some, but it is necessary for success in innovation.

It's also worth mentioning that in order to succeed in Silicon Valley, innovators must find opportunities to solve widely experienced problems and design solutions and messages that address those needs. As an innovator, it's important to ask yourself what your internal target market needs on their success journey and to be passionate about helping them succeed.

Ultimately, the success journey of the employee is the key to great innovations and bottom-line value. As an OI coach, your job is to help innovators understand the needs of their internal market (other people in the organisation with the same problem) and develop solutions that meet those needs.

By focusing on the needs of your employee innovator's internal market and providing meaningful coaching, you can unlock extraordinary OI opportunities and drive real value for your organization. Silicon Valley has become synonymous with success, but what is it that sets these iconic companies apart? The answer lies in their focus on helping people be successful at something, rather than simply addressing perceived problems. This approach involves strategy and empathy, and it's what we call "The Success Journey of the Employee."

5

BOOTSTRAPPING FOR SUCCESS

Silicon Valley is known for its continuous grind for startup traction, but you don't have to come to the Valley to learn how it works. In this chapter, we'll explore the lessons learned from my 'hacker-hostel' in Mountain View and how they can be applied to any OI innovator's search for success.

Before achieving real customers and a legitimate business opportunity, money and investor interest are scarce. This is where bootstrapping comes in. The founder or co-founders have to self-fund their startup, requiring serious financial bootstrapping to build the innovation and identify the market while distinguishing themselves in a crowded startup scene. This phase is known as the 'Seed Stage', and it's essential to understand the early-stage phase of well-known startups like Airbnb or Uber. By looking at their origins, we can learn how they started with no serious capital or a clear idea of what their product would eventually be.

In OI, if we can get to a demo prototype of whatever the OI is, we're starting on the right foot without having to get money from a budget. Even a demo to prove it can solve the problem at scale and meets the employee and the team's needs will validate the innovation opportunity sufficiently to get management interest and budget to make it happen. This is how Silicon Valley works: doing seed-stage innovation without money, grinding forward, gaining traction in developing a scalable solution to solve a common problem.

The essence of this message for organizations wanting to develop radical new ways of working is this: budget processes are stodgy at best. An implemented pilot or working demo creating efficiencies in a team, and ultimately a better employee experience, proves business value better than a slide deck. The beta, an OI that has been deployed to a small group of employees, has to prove its ROI value will beat the internal rate of capital return or IRR of the organization.

Once proven, and internal politics aside, getting support will be a lot easier. After the prototype has been in play, sufficiently long enough to have established its adequacy, data can be collected about its impact. Using this data will result in a meaningful business case, which, if positive, improves the chances of getting investment from a budget.

But why do we need to innovate and create bottom-line value? Money is, in part, a motivator for the individual OI Innovator, just as it is, in part, in Silicon Valley. Why shouldn't employee innovators be rewarded for a great OI? OI Coaches can establish policies to financially reward their OI Innovators who took an innovation through the OI Value Chain and created wealth for the organization.

Learning from Silicon Valley, we know that success is a poor teacher, and the best way to achieve success is to fail often and fail hard. But this failure *can* lead to meaning and reward, if good OI coaches are in place. By applying the lessons learned and coaching OI, we can create a new way to radically design, transform, and scale new ways of working for organizations worldwide.

6

YOU CAN CHANGE THE WORLD

In this chapter, we explore the fundamental aspect of an innovator's mindset - the belief that one can change the world. As OI Coaches, we approach potential innovators with the message that they have the power to make a difference, not just within the organization but beyond. Steve Jobs was a master at messaging, and he made people believe that having a Mac was a part of the journey to making the world a better place.

In marketing Silicon Valley innovations, the message is everything, and it has to be right to ensure maximum awareness and understanding of the solution. But it's not just about the message - the product has to be good enough to be widely adopted. When coaching OI, we focus on developing a story that employees relate to and want to adopt intrinsically.

Empathy is a crucial element of coaching OI. We need to understand our employees' Success Journeys and help them achieve personal success in the workplace. By creating a conversational space where employees can talk about their goals and aspirations, we can be the bedrock for their work Success Journey. As OI Coaches, we must continuously dig deeper into what the innovator is trying to achieve and how it will support both their Success Journey and the organization's objectives.

In Silicon Valley, experienced investor guidance is generally welcomed by the innovator. But to be successful requires validation and traction with customers, requiring grit, discipline, and consistency. Successful innovators need to focus on their coworker's Success Journey needs and their team's needs to create more value through innovation. This focus will become a part of the human innovation platform culture.

Empathy is an incredible tool in growing our connected human consciousness, developing a stronger social organization. It might be the most essential aspect of one's self to develop. OI Coaches need to understand everything is about others and how to help them on their Success Journeys.

That's their value proposition when coaching OI, assisting people with their Success Journeys, and them, the Success Journeys of others.

In conclusion, the belief that we can change the world is an essential aspect of an innovator's mindset. As OI Coaches, we need to develop empathy and focus on other's success to be effective in coaching OI. By helping employees achieve personal success in the workplace, we can create value for both the organization and the innovator. With empathy and focus, we can create a human innovation platform culture that drives innovation and solves the problems of others.

7

STRATEGIZING FOR SUCCESS IN ORGANIZATIONAL INNOVATION

In order to activate the interest of employees to become OI Innovators, a CEO might consider launching an awareness campaign about the organization's OI aspirations. This campaign should be followed up by more detailed communications from executives and team-leads. Up to 15% of employees could respond positively and request consideration for selection as an OI Innovator. Managers are ideally positioned in organizations to be great OI Coaches and, with a little support and training, can support the organization to start doing OI actively.

The first step for an OI Coach working with an OI Innovator is to facilitate an exercise to define an innovation game-plan or strategies. This process leads to a deeper relationship with the employee innovator, making the idea of a more profound purpose more real. As the employee unpacks their ideas for progressing their Success Journey, the idea of a more profound purpose may arise and become the innovator's OI Mission.

The OI Coach facilitates the OI Innovator's mission story, using deep empathy and support. The mission story could be as simple as: "Achieving brilliant Accounts Payable operations and stakeholder experiences." With more discussion, specific themes become evident. These are all important in setting the building blocks of the OI Innovator's strategy or strategies.

Sharing the innovator's strategy with impacted business leaders and getting their input and support will greatly help the organization's innovation culture. Each Success Journey strategy includes goals. Planning the achievement of these goals, through identifying activities, then the challenges and ways to overcome them, help make the approach more practical to execute.

When facilitating an exercise that helps define the innovator's strategies, the OI Coach does a SWOT analysis with the innovator. This exercise means looking at an innovator's strategic opportunities and threats, then determining what strengths to leverage to meet some opportunity. Conversely, identifying the weaknesses that need strengthening to prevent some threat.

An innovator's strategy should be straightforward. In publishing this book, our strategy is:
To use our knowledge (strength) of how Silicon Valley businesses innovate, to meet a global need (opportunity) of readers wanting to learn how to develop radically better ways of working.

A game plan (vision) creates the context for a strategy, which in our case is:
To write and publish about a scaleable innovation and coaching framework.

The purpose (mission) driving all this is:
To achieve worldwide adoption of OI.

A strategy's origin is always the 'Why?'. Pieces that make up a complete definition of what an organization is about start with Purpose (Mission), then Game-Plan (Vision), followed by the Strategy, Strategic Goals, and Strategic Needs.

In the workplace, an OI coach needs to know an employee's strategic goals through a strategy discussion. An OI Coach will have to be able to assess the needs of the team and help the innovator to set personal strategic goals. Once the innovator's goals are set, the coach might discover opportunities to support the innovator in overcoming challenges or finding opportunities to achieve those goals.

OI isn't about ideas. It's about problems. Innovation starts by understanding the problem and the scale of the problem, for other people. In the first OI coaching session with an OI Innovator, the coach talks about why they want to do it. The coach should identify the innovator's problem and how many other employees are experiencing the same problem. The design of the solution will often change in the ideation phase as the problem becomes better understood.

Competing key-stakeholder agendas, argued within the context of a functional silo, not within the context of a cross-departmental value-chain, are toxic to the organization's mission. For organizations to be effective, the leadership of an organization needs to break down functional silos. Executives leading these functions need to align their operational management, integrating with other functions, supporting value creation in an end-to-end value-chain.

The OI Innovator's role is to help other employees in their Success Journeys. Deeply understanding the needs of others and having a workable solution to a common problem is enough to start calculating the feasibility of the design. Game plans can be great when simple, easy enough to communicate and inspire enough to be a daily driving force behind a product, a team, and a business.

8

FINANCIAL FEASIBILITY

The OI "Pitch" or "Business Case" ultimately determines whether to pursue a project or not. Similar to the Shark Tank TV show, senior managers and executives pitch the business case for their Capital Expenditure and Operating Expenditure budgets (CAPEX and OPEX). They must achieve the business goals for their division or department for the next year and demonstrate budget and operational plan variances by quarter, sometimes by month.

However, from the perspective of an OI Innovator, it is challenging to state how they understand the financial impacts of an OI. The OI Innovator might not want to start the OI Innovation process because calculating the feasibility is an administrative task that few will enjoy. Few enjoy working out the details of an organization's potential for extra value and how to achieve it, unless they get part of it. Sales teams get financially rewarded with sales commissions for creating value through customer sales. Why shouldn't an innovator get innovation commission on the value their innovation achieves?

To calculate the potential value of an innovation, Silicon Valley starts with what dreamers and high-level thinkers calculate and get excited about, called the "Top-Down" view (Total Addressable Market or TAM). Then there's what will either be the rocket that blows up the founder's dreams or the rocket that will launch them into the stratosphere called "Bottom-Up" (Serviceable Obtainable Market or SOM). SOM is the part of the identified market who actually have the pain (Serviceable Available Market or SAM).

Firstly, there's the easy part: Top-Down: Total Addressable Market (TAM). This is normally the job of the marketing department, getting market insights into which target organizations (B2B) or consumer profiles (B2C) best fit the characteristics of having the identified problem. TAM is fun! This is where the innovator's heart will race and their eyes shine.

For example, suppose you have gone through a cinema user experience design session with a few cinema customers and realized that there seems to be a common need with cinema customers for a movie ticket holder. This meets a need, a pain point, that when people go to a cinema complex, they can carry their popcorn and drink without trying to balance one on their forearm whilst they reach for their movie ticket. As a solution to this widely-experienced problem, you design a ticket holder, made from bamboo, which is a cup-sized ring that fits around your drink cup and you can clip your ticket into this ticket holder, so you can hold your popcorn and drink, with your tickets clipped into your bamboo ticket holder. You trademark this invention as the 'TickyRing'.

Now we understand the pain point and product solution design, let's calculate the TAM.

At least one report says that 1.68 Billion people go to movies annually around the world (2011). We can keep that figure the same for 2023, because although the global population is growing, COVID-19 and online movie services like Netflix, and increasingly expensive ticket pricing means cinema attendance as a percentage of population is on the decline. To continue our TAM calculation, we price our ticket holder at $5 (it's organic, responsibly-grown bamboo). So our Total Addressable Market is $8.25 Billion.

However, to put this data into a Pitch (Business Case), you need to start with these figures from your TAM, SAM, and

SOM calculations. Then you need to show data, in other words, how many people, based on research you've done, have this pain point (SAM) are within your reach and would buy a ticket holder (SOM). You'd also have to design the ticket holder, patent it, trademark it, etc. These setup and project costs need to be factored into your pitch.

Ultimately you want to scale your innovation, which means rolling it out to people who have the same problem. You have to do this SAM and SOM calculation and be clear about how you are going to achieve that figure using Scale Plans which is how you get to your customers. The same applies to the OI Feasibility study within an organization. The OI Innovator, when being coached OI, will detail how the targeted employees will adapt to the OI in the organization and what the top or bottom line benefits are going to be, thereby generating, in simple terms, the OI business case and ROI for a specific innovation.

A similar approach can be taken for new products and services for customers. The Business Case or Pitch Deck will help to partly answer the OI Feasibility question. Our innovation platform we call 'icntr' makes calculating this business case easy. It keeps track of the investment performance across the OI Value Chain.

To summarize, the OI "Pitch" or "Business Case" ultimately determines whether to invest in the OI, or not. Calculating the feasibility is an administrative task that few will enjoy, but it is necessary to understand the financial impacts of an OI. Silicon Valley starts with the "Top-Down" view (Total Addressable Market or TAM) and then the "Bottom-Up" view (Serviceable Obtainable Market or SOM) to calculate the potential value of an innovation. The Business Case or Pitch Deck will help to answer the OI Feasibility question, and our innovation platform 'icntr' makes calculating this business case super easy.

9

THE INVESTOR'S PERSPECTIVE

If you were to search for venture capital in Palo Alto using any maps app, you will see hundreds of dots appearing in a relatively small location. This area, the heart of Silicon Valley, is geographically more or less the center between San Francisco and San Jose, running along the western shore of the San Francisco Bay. Venture capitalists, or VCs, are in the business of funneling funds from registered investors or institutes into selected startups.

Some of these investors are wealthy individuals, investing their own funds (Angel Investors), while others are people posing as investors only to see what the startup is working on. Some of these fake venture capitalists serve foreign nations' interests, sharing the latest and most significant innovation decks in Silicon Valley with their friends back home. It is crucial to research whom you are sending your pitch deck to and not trust anybody you do not know.

From the perspective of genuine investors, disruptive innovations do not have a market yet or provable value that could be added to the bottom line. Hence, there is no future data upon which to make an investment decision. According to Christensen in his book, The Innovator's Dilemma, investors use two acid tests to ascertain if there is a market or not. Firstly, VC's make decisions based on recent technology trends. The fourth industrial revolution includes drones, AI, robotics, the Internet of Things (IoT), autonomous vehicles, etc. Consequently, VC's are investing almost exclusively in innovations that include these latest technologies. Whether or not an organization will take the same investment principles in terms of what technologies to use within the organization depends on how well OI is working in the organization to identify internal use-cases for these technologies.

The second trick investors use is only to invest where there is researched data on who has the problem described by the innovator, known as a 'use-case.' Data showing clear needs get investors in Silicon Valley excited. The same should happen in organizations. Where OI reveals problems, solutions, and bottom-line value, should excite all of management. Essentially, every organizational manager, at all levels, is a Venture Capitalist.

They are either making resource allocations to keep things as they are, or they are allocating part of their resources to building the future. Only the latter will result in sustainable future returns.

Developing ideas into reality but not focusing on how it's going to meet current or future organizational needs, based on which employees currently have specific pains, is a gamble. Budget won't be given to an OI without OI Feasibility and Design Value Mapping analysis being done with some significant measure of confidence in that data and the potential for creating value, with a set of issues, risks, and assumptions clearly articulated - the details matter!

In an organization using OI, coaches can keep data on our icntr system, on hand or memorized, about specific OIs. An OI Coach can use icntr like a hedge-fund manager watching their investment portfolio. Suppose a coach is walking around the organization's campus with clipboards, virtual or otherwise, always with OI data in hand. In that case, it makes for effective casual standup OI chats and encounters, much like Agile coaches manage their development teams. project or not. Calculating the feasibility is an administrative task that few will enjoy, but it is necessary to understand the financial impacts of an OI. Silicon Valley starts with the

"Top-Down" view (Total Addressable Market or TAM) and then the "Bottom-Up" view (Serviceable Obtainable Market or SOM) to calculate the potential value of an innovation. The Business Case or Pitch Deck will help to answer the OI Feasibility question, using our innovation platform 'icntr' can help with this.

10

DESIGN

In the world of business, success hinges on the ability to create something that people want to use. To achieve this, it's crucial to understand the decision-making process of consumers. People make up their minds quickly and are unlikely to change their minds once they've made a decision. Ultimately, the question that people ask themselves is whether or not a product can easily do what they want it to do. This is why a product's value proposition is so important.

Innovation is all about creating something that solves a problem or fulfills a need. This is what we call the Pain, Gain, Help motivators. To achieve this, it's essential to focus on the design of the product. The design should be easy to use and should be able to help other employees in their day-to-day tasks. This is where the OI Innovator comes in. Their job is to identify pain points and create innovative solutions that can help the organization.

Before any design work can begin, it's vital to understand the needs of the person or organization. This is where data comes in. Steve Jobs was a master at using data to drive his decision-making process. The same can be said for Tim Cook, who has continued Apple's success by using data to improve the supply chain and retail operations. It's crucial to innovate internally and continuously improve how the organization runs.

To create a successful innovation, it's essential to understand the Success Journey of the employee. This involves understanding their personal goals and how they believe they can innovate to create value for the organization. The OI Coach and Innovator can have great conversations to unpack effective solutions, and a single solution idea may cascade into many levels of concepts.

The key to designing a great product is to make sure that the OI Innovator understands the organization's Success Journey and the strategic goals. This will help them identify where OI can help attain some strategic goal, such as profit. The OI Coach and Innovator need to go completely right-brained and use informational interviews to understand where employees have real growth issues.

Innovation is all about delivering a great product or service experience to the market. Simplicity is critical in OI, and it's essential not to deliver more than what the internal market needs. The focus should be on developing a great product or service experience that can sustain a feeling of continuous enjoyment in using the product. Stanford University Design School videos are a great resource for understanding the design process better.

In conclusion, innovation is all about creating something that solves a problem or fulfills a need. To achieve this, it's essential to focus on the design of the product and understand the needs of the person or organization. By doing this, the OI Innovator can create innovative solutions that can help the organization achieve its strategic goals, by meeting the needs of the employee's Success Journey.

11

TRANSFORM

Transformation in OI is the process of taking a design and making it real. However, in many organizations, it can be a challenging task. An OI can improve any aspect of an organization, such as budget policy, system control, or job procedure. Digital Transformation contains many OIs that help transform manual processes into digital ones, using modern ERP technologies.

The book 'Digital Core' explains that every real-world occurrence has the potential for a digital twin. This concept presents opportunities for new products and services. Recent digital strategies are looking at how the Internet of Things, AI, and software robotics can drive immense OI value, with first-movers potentially getting an advantage over their competitors.

The key to validating an OI is prototyping. Teams should

start small and simple, test it, and build on the lessons learned. This simple approach will create a more efficient path to ultimate success. Agile Project Management says the same thing. Get the requirement, sprint to build it, then show and take the feedback, repeat.

Whereas OI primarily focuses on the essence of transformation, the innovation that drives it, and the plans to scale it to the internal market. Are IT project teams clear on what aspects of business they are transforming and against what business ambitions? Arguably not.

Real transformation is generally the combination of action and managing the impact of that action. In an OI, we have to consider the transformation we are making and the actions and impact chain we need to manage to make that change happen.

An OI requires detailed planning to get it ready for others. Managing OI Transformation is different from managing for example, a digital transformation. In OI, identifying impacts and de-risking business readiness for the impact are as important as the delivery task causing the impact. Both are part of a business-owned 'Business Action'.
There's no project team in OI.

Every Transformation Action and Transformation Impact, paired as a Business Action, can have chains of sub-activities related to either completing some action AND addressing some impact. Every action has an impact. It's up to the innovator, supported by the coach, to find out what they are. To prepare the impacted stakeholders, whether the impact is a pain or a gain. Also, to calculate what that effort will cost: 'ACTION + IMPACT.' This rolls up to the OI Business Case and feasibility.

The OI's potential to create transformation in people's lives so that they can achieve their success requires detailed attention to the actions and impact chain. Every action has an impact, and it's crucial to consider and manage them. This is why we introduce 'Business Actions' instead of Project Management in OI. The impacts identified as part of a typical Change Impact Analysis (CIA) of delivery actions in typical project plans are considered, but are too high level. Or the CIA spreadsheet or tracker, is part of a deliverable in a phase in the middle of a project, and don't consider the final design and what is eventually built and deployed. This makes one of the many weaknesses of using Project Management theory for transforming businesses and running IT projects. In conclusion, OI requires detailed planning, consideration of impacts, and managing the actions and impact chain, at a detailed level. With a focus on managing OI Transformation, it's possible to create a more efficient path to ultimate success.

12

SCALE

As you continue on your journey to uncover the best-kept secrets of Silicon Valley, it's important to reflect on what you've learned so far. This chapter will focus on the final stage of the OI Value Chain: how to SCALE.

Recall the three steps of the OI Value Chain: DESIGN, TRANSFORM, and SCALE. The DESIGN and TRANSFORM processes are irrelevant without measurable value in the OI being used by others with the same problem. The SCALE Plans are the steps to identify the value of rolling out the product or service into the organization.

Scaling innovations that solve employees' job problems need to be support the organisation's objectives too. Employees creating value with the OI should contribute to the bottom-up OI Business Case. In this OI Value Chain step 'SCALE', the OI Innovator needs to get to the detail where the real value is unlocked, where people are having the problem. The OI value comes from the number of people using the OI per SCALE Plan, multiplied by the value per person using the OI.

Assuming there are 5,000 account payable clerks, and this OI saves each person a day's worth of effort every month, with an average cost of $150 per person per day, the total saving value generated by this OI would be $750,000 per month (calculated as 5000 x $150).

OI Innovators start with big numbers, top-down, but always ask themselves what the TRANSFORM business actions and SCALE Plans are to achieve the total planned OI value. The innovator will need to keep drilling down into the plan to roll out the OI, collecting as much value and cost detail as possible. This will improve the quality of the Business Case. The first Scale Plan is generally the product 'Beta' (first tested, working product).

Detailed SCALE Plans will ensure the business case continuously calibrates with reality. Well-defined stakeholder-groups that will use the OI and are mapped to specific SCALE Plans help generate useful financial reports about the OI. With SCALE Plans, we aim to detail impact value.

To create high impact innovation value, we have to either make something much cheaper than a current thing or introduce something to a new market who didn't have it before. Innovators are encouraged by coaches to make a difference, to change the world and OI Coaches inspire OI Innovators to help the organization succeed in new ways.

Getting back to TickyRing (the movie ticket holder we introduced as an example innovation), we can communicate via a website, educate through a video, and train through the same video how it works. Getting people to adopt an innovation requires a plan to communicate, educate and train, in that order, assessing where they are after each step while making sure each step is timely and comprehensible in relation to their need. During the DESIGN phase of the OI Value Chain, it is important to identify the needs of employees. This ensures that communication is effective, as concepts related to problems or areas where help is required are conveyed to individuals who are already familiar with them. This approach is essential for success of the OI and is also the recommended process to follow for any Organizational Change Management. The problem is, in traditional transformations, the pains of the employees are seldom considered. This is why so much is invested in using change management to reinforce some new way of working, or a new system. OI Solves the employee's problems.

Now that we've outlined OI's foundation, we'll introduce some of Silicon Valley's most famous people and look at why they are so revered. Then we'll ask, who at your organization could have similar characteristics and be drivers of OI where you work. Could it be you? Read on to see who you are most similar to.

13

MAKING IT HAPPEN

"Just one more thing..."
Steve Jobs

Before we dive into the importance of making innovation work, let me share a valuable lesson I learned from a friend in the Valley. He tells his adult kids, "Don't f*** it up," a phrase he picked up from Silicon Valley legend, Bill Campbell. In the book 'Trillion-Dollar Coach,' Bill is portrayed as the most admired business coach in Silicon Valley, and his famous expression has an entire chapter dedicated to it. It's crucial advice for anyone looking to succeed, as one mistake could cost a lot of money.

Once an OI Business Case is accepted, and budget finances start flowing, the OI Innovator must work hard and smart enough to keep the OI Business Case on track. If they mess up, it could mean that much of the money goes to waste. The innovator must stick to the Business Case numbers, do what they have to in order to comply with the plan, and control financial feasibility variance by setting the target and working incessantly towards it. In short, they must not f*** it up!

But how do you ensure that you're on track? It's essential to drill down into the corporate strategy and the underlying intentions to keep the OI delivering value against the organization's objectives. The innovator must keep their eye on the ball, live, sleep, and breathe their objectives to keep their OI in demand and the numbers on track.

When launching a new brand, it's easy to get carried away and mess up the message to people. We need to focus on the other person, their challenges, and what they think can solve the problem. A simple approach to conversations can go a long way in people wanting to know more, and employees wanting to use the OI, a solution to their problems, thus keeping on track with the numbers.

From an OI Operations perspective, OI Innovators and Coaches should implement and manage the OI processes, report on the numbers, and stay on track, whatever that takes. If the OI Prototype isn't working or the messaging is wrong, then the OI Design and message may need to pivot in another direction.

In conclusion, making innovation work is not about the 'us', but about what it does for the other person. So, don't f*** it up! Keep your eye on the ball, stay focused on your objectives, and keep the numbers on track. That's how you make it happen, and like Jobs, will always have that one more thing that'll blow people's minds.

14

SILICON VALLEY MENTORS

It's challenging to stay on the numbers, not to mess things up. This challenge to stay on track is why mentors, heroes, inspiring pioneers, and Silicon Valley investors are so essential to learn from. We wanted to introduce different types of hero mentors and leaders some of the best the valley have (or had). People who have guided and coached massively successful business founders and CEO's. While reading about these people, we suggest that you try to identify people within your organization who might share similar character traits. These heroes understood the Success Journey principles and applied them to their leadership and coaching roles. The Global Silicon Valley's Hall of Fame inductees inspire this chapter. Large corporations could learn a lot from these people and find that they have their own heroes, ready and willing to create a mini Silicon Valley inside their organizations.

Larry Sonsini

Larry is a counsel to tech titans. Ideas can be copied, partnerships can be botched, investment deals can go sideways, quick. He's the goto guy to make sure none of this stuff happens. He has been a special advisor to Steve Jobs, Elon Musk, Google, HP and many others. He is one of the most respected people in Silicon Valley. Whilst he is a lawyer, he goes so much further in building relationships of care and integrity. He's the guy who gets deals done, properly.

Dick Kramlich

Dick is a trailblazer in the Venture Capital arena in Silicon Valley. His understanding of people, software and investing proves he's a role model in Silicon Valley. He really helps to nurture founders. Even competitors admire and respect how he makes business decisions combining deep technical understanding and recognizing the potential of founders. At 80 years old he's still a wonderful source of industry knowledge and very much involved in supporting and building founders and portfolios. He is most well known for his integrity.

Bill 'Coach' Campbell (Read Trillion Dollar Coach!)

Bill had such a deep background in Silicon Valley, he is easily recognized as the biggest name in CEO coaching circles. He has helped Apple, Google in the early days, in fact, there are few massive Silicon Valley successes that do not have his direct influence somewhere. He is the ultimate coach to CEOs and founders. Investors and founders speak of him with such deep esteem, it is likely no other person gets as much recognition, as being a mentor in developing some of the best business leaders in the world.

Diane Green

Diane's courage to think different started virtualization at VMWare which is now the bedrock of cloud computing, globally. A pretty big impact on the world! She led VMWare to be one of the biggest software companies. She inspires founders to think different, to speak truthfully and not be shy to take big steps into unknown territories.

Mike Homer

Mike played major technology leadership roles in Silicon Valley's software world. From building Netscape, to developing the world's most recognized software technologies. Some say he was the person who set the bar in what software was capable of, and inspired so many to reach that bar. He is described as being incredibly caring of people, but always driving people to push the limits of software. Crazy smart, he would always do the right thing for the people around him.

Ken Coleman

Ken participates on numerous boards even in today's Silicon Valley. He pioneered mentoring in tech startups and has led many himself. He is considered one of the most genuinely caring people in Silicon Valley and is such an iconic hero people speak of him as one of the valley's greats. Specializing in sales and service, he led one of the toughest areas of business in such a way as to be the example of how to tackle the most difficult area of startups, getting customers.

Andy Grove

Andy essentially, led Intel into its biggest growth period ever, setting records for businesses around the world. He grew intel from $4 Billion a year, to over $200 Billion a year. He is considered the best business leader of all time.

Gordy Davidson

Gordy is considered the best of trusted advisors in the area of public offerings. He has taken all the Silicon Valley greats from privately owned to public. He has worked on the biggest mergers in the valley too. He took WhatsApp to Facebook for $19 Billion, the largest acquisition of a private company, of all time. Given the fact that Silicon Valley is a hotbed of investing for the sake of exits as either public or mergers, he is loved for his ability to make people wealthy. He is known as the guy to trust, to get a deal done.

Carol Bartz

Finally, Carol Bartz blazed into the Silicon Valley scene as an executive at Sun Microsystems and CEO of AutoDesk, turning it into one of the most profitable companies in the valley.

These heroes understood the Success Journey principles and applied them to their leadership and coaching roles. Their stories offer valuable lessons for any business leader looking to achieve success. So, take a page from their book and identify people within your own organization who share similar character traits. Large corporations could learn a lot from these people and find that they have their own mentors, ready and willing to create a mini Silicon Valley inside their organizations.

15

SILICON VALLEY HEROES

The mentors mentioned previously are just some of the people yesterday's startup founders had to lean on for guidance and mentoring. It's important to understand also, that Silicon Valley is not just about tech, it's a lot about people. Silicon Valley is experienced as a very difficult place to be successful. Issues such as diversity make it more so, and when talking about pioneers, we also need to acknowledge people who pioneer aspects of society in the Valley.

Their dollar value grows every day...

Sheryl Sandberg
Financial Worth 1.61 billion USD

Sheryl is a big deal, I mean a really big deal. For starters her boss is Mark Zuckerberg and she runs arguably one of the biggest operations, for one of the most well-known brands on the planet. As COO for Facebook, she has fought gender discrimination and won. She wrote a great book, inspiring millions of women around the world. 'Lean In' sold 140,000 copies in its first week. That's insane! Not only is she an amazing boss and author, but also a speaker. She always draws a large crowd and is one of the valley's biggest inspirations, for all.

Mark Benioff

Financial Worth $ 7.7 billion USD

Mark got into cloud-computing and made it famous long before anyone else. The challenge with cloud is security, privacy, connection reliability, amongst others. When he started Salesforce with co-founder Parker Harris, he fought the odds with a vision so strong, that it broke the mold of on-premise enterprise solutions. He is a strong advocate for diversity and is an admired and trusted business leader. His staff number 25,000 and the Salesforce head office in San Francisco City is really nice. His showmanship and absolute positive focus makes him a great business leader. He held Steve Jobs in the highest regard, as an inspiration and mentor.

Hasso Platner
Financial Worth 9.1 billion USD

Hasso is one of the founders of SAP, originally a German startup, it transferred to the US, where Hasso has been extremely active in Silicon Valley since early 2000's. His name is on the Stanford University Design School, the very institution that spread 'design-thinking' around the world. His work in Silicon Valley shows he's still a very active founder and has been driving change within SAP's architecture for some time. Always looking for ways to help business run better using SAP software.

SAP Is the largest provider of ERP Business Software, in the world.

Elon Musk
Financial Worth 188 billion USD

Elon to me, epitomizes the startup founder. He sets himself solid missions, develops visions to achieve that purpose and leads execution like very few other founders and CEO's can. He arguably co-founded Tesla, certainly was responsible for building it into one of the most admired businesses in the world. He started SpaceX, vastly reducing the cost of space transportation and has set a goal to lead humanity, in becoming a multi-planetary species.

He talks casually but very intellectually. Elon will be playing a big role in AI and brain interfacing technology.

Here's an example of his leadership: I noticed a Tesla customer complaining to him on twitter, that other Tesla customers were abusing car charging bays by parking in them, to avoid driving around full parking areas, looking for parking. He was pretty annoyed about this, and later that day I saw him in the Palo Alto city hall parking garage assessing who was parking in the Tesla charging bays. He likes to solve problems asap. If you're interested, Ashlee Vance, one of my coffee machine colleagues in Palo Alto, wrote a superb biography about Elon Musk, being one of the few to actually get quality time with Elon to do this.

BTW, Elon played a tiny roll in the second Iron Man Movie, asking Tony Stark to meet about an Electric Car startup.

Elon has a real sense of humor, although less so these days with the risk of AI, he is working hard to get the right controls in place to prevent malicious AI. It makes him pretty nervous.

Mark Zuckerberg
Financial Worth 77.1 billion USD

Founder of Facebook, Mark has more money than he cares to have, which is why he and his wife have started the Chan Zuckerberg Initiative (CZI) to give away 99% of it. His startup history is only a little blurry when you consider just how blurry startup history can be. He has built an awesome company together with Sheryl Sandberg. The Facebook head office is easily one of the most stunning work places I have ever seen. He constantly challenges his teams to do more, to provide a better product.

I accidentally nearly knocked over Mark's 3-year-old daughter with a new broom handle I was carrying. Then I saw her alarmed dad, Mark looking at me with a pretty fierce, "Careful, that's my daughter!" look. Feeling like an idiot, I apologized and moved on...just another jeans and t-shirt kinda dad.

Larry Page, Sergey Brin

Financial Worth: Larry $ 93 Billion USD, Sergey $ 89 Billion

Larry and Sergey are the founders of Google and more recently, Alphabet, a new business that owns Google and invests in new startups.

Alphabet is valued at upwards of $ 600 Billion, at one point in 2016, it was valued at more than Apple, the most valuable company in the world.

These two are sometimes seen around Silicon Valley and when they are, people talk about them like the legends they are. I saw Sergey once and he seemed a cool guy.

Steve Jobs
Financial Worth $ *127 Billion USD (Apple is worth $3 Trillion)

Silicon Valley has a love/hate relationship with Steve. Most love him, those who worked with him don't. With few exceptions, two of them are Apple's head designer, Jony Ivy, and the man who took over from Steve as CEO, Tim Cook.

*At the time of Steve's passing, he was worth around $ 10 Billion. But if he had held onto his Apple shares, instead of selling them when he was 'fired' from Apple, his fortune would be worth $127 Billion now. There is so much on the net about him that you could research. Inspired, I used to sit in an empty property next door to his humble Palo Alto home eating Apples from the trees he planted in front of his house. What can I say? ...I like Apples.

16

SILICON VALLEY INVESTORS

There are different types of investors in the valley. For example, institutional investors, like IBM investing in a startup, or internal product. Then there's Venture Capital firms, such as Sequoia Capital. There's Angel Investors such as Ron Conway, there's family trust investment firms, investing on behalf of a wealthy family, and then there are those with cash to spare and the courage to invest in startups. Probably the most important thing to learn about investment deals, is the stage of the startup and how the investment is done. Typically, investment deals are talked about using the terms, 'Seed', 'Late Seed', 'Series A, B,C,D' and on a rare occasion 'E Round' which describe the phase a startup is in.

Marc Andreessen, co-founder of Netscape and Andreessen Horowitz, one of the biggest VC's in the valley, talks about these different investment rounds as risk mitigation strategies. He says that in the seed round, a startup should be building the team, the product and beta-testing, so seed money or seed investment is to remove the obstacles to do that. Series A, should be about getting the first paying customers, A Round funding should be sufficient to get the marketing right and start selling. Series B, and the rest, is all about scaling the business, and the funding to scale.

These investors have a real knack for spotting talented founders with a strong focus on what people legitimately need, they can spot fake needs a mile away! They primarily invest in the market opportunity, not how great a founder is, or how intelligent the product may be. I think there's scope in existing businesses to take the approach of Silicon Valley investors when it comes to budgeting and business cases for their Organizational Innovations. It is done to a degree, but could be improved substantially.

Let's look at some of the valley's greatest investors and firms.

Roelof Botha

Financial Worth $300 Million USD

Roelof more or less runs Sequoia Capital and owns four Tesla's. Yes, he's a close friend of Elon. They worked together at PayPal, Roelof as CFO. He sits on the boards of most of Silicon Valley's more recent successes, such as MongoDB. He also just recently started playing a more prominent leadership role at Sequoia, where Doug Leone is likely grooming Roelof for CEO position. Sequoia Capital is iconic in the valley. Doug and previous CEO, Michael Moritz, both deserve further studying. Roelof is a really great guy! IMHO Nobody is as smart, has as much money, and more humility and good grace, than him.

Ron Conway
Financial Worth $ 1.5 Billion USD

Ron is described as a 'Super Angel'. He is incredibly well connected in the valley and does a lot, meaning, actively gets involved in social development and financially supports many charities in San Francisco. I had the chance to meet him and pitch our app. His team are more focussed on networking apps not so much enterprise apps like ours. I was sent a well mannered regret.

He is the original Silicon Valley Angel Investor.

Peter Thiel
Financial Worth $ 4.2 Billion USD

Peter invested in a lot of the right startups. His own startup experience was together with Elon and Roelof at PayPal where they worked together and succeeded together. He has very strong political convictions, being the biggest rare Silicon Valley supporter of Donald Trump's presidency. He has enormous influence in the valley.

17

YOUR SUCCESS JOURNEY

As a business leader interested in coaching OI, you likely have a basic understanding of what OI is about and how it can lead to success, much like the mentors and heroes of Silicon Valley. But let's revisit the OI Value Chain and its three essential steps: Design, Transform, and Scale.

To further understand the value of these steps, let's look at some advice from successful Silicon Valley leaders. Steve Jobs once said that "People with passion can change the world for the better," which aligns perfectly with the Design step of creating a better world. Larry Page emphasized the importance of combining invention and innovation with commercialization and getting products to people, which reflects the Transform and Scale steps of the OI Value Chain.

Elon Musk advised entrepreneurs to try and sell their product or service to real customers to generate momentum, which again speaks to the importance of the Scale step of the OI Value Chain.

Now, it's time to start your own Success Journey by focusing on the needs of others and establishing your market size. The OI Value Chain can help you do this. First, identify who you are designing for and their purpose, game-plan, strategy, and strategic goals and needs. Then, design a solution that addresses these needs.

Next, describe the transformation necessary to turn your solution into a reality and manage any impacts. Plan actions and managing their impacts, and costs of these business-owned activities. Finally, describe how you will test and pilot your solution in a real-world situation and get employees onboard through communication, education, and training.

To determine the investment business case, calculate your TAM, SAM, and SOM, as well as your transformation costs and total profits from sales. Deduct your total transformation costs from your profits to determine your total profit and ROI. Finally, consider the rate of return and decide whether to proceed or start again.

Yes, the Success Journey is not easy, but trying will make it easier. Use the OI Value Chain to guide your journey and achieve success.

18

INTRODUCING THE OI MANAGEMENT PRINCIPLES

Could OI coaching be a step change in the evolution of the manager role?

Many business students are familiar with Henri Fayol's four management functions: Plan, Lead, Organize, and Control. However, we propose an adjustment to align with the needs of managers who wish to become OI Coaches. In this chapter, we explore the idea of coaching OI as a new management role and encourage all managers to become OI Coaches. We present these principles, laid over traditional management functions, to guide OI coaching:

1. Strategize (Team SWOT Analysis & Mapping)
2. Lead (Mission, Vision, Culture, Motivation)
3. Transform (Transcend+Transition)
4. Coach (Supporting the team to achieve goals)

As we follow the OI Value Chain of DESIGN, TRANSFORM, SCALE, we can see that coaching OI involves helping teams manage each step of the OI Value Chain. Each section requires strategizing, leadership, transformation, and coaching.

	DESIGN	TRANSFORM	SCALE
Strategize	1.1 Activities	2.1 Activities	3.1 Activities
Lead	1.2 Activities	2.2 Activities	3.2 Activities
Transform	1.3 Activities	2.3 Activitiies	3.3 Activities
Coach	1.4 Activities	2.4 Activities	3.4 Activities

OI Coaching Matrix

To understand how to manage OI Value Chain activities, refer to the matrix in the table above. In this chapter, we focus on the DESIGN step and its various functions.

1. DESIGN

1.1 DESIGN: Strategize

When coaching OI, it's essential to understand the employee's mission, vision, and strategy. The OI Coach can contribute to the OI Innovator's strategy work by guiding how relevant the strategy may be in relation to the team's strategy and goals. Enterprise systems can provide meaningful data, and through analysis of this data, OI Coaches can gather insights about things that might be of value to the innovator.

1.2 DESIGN: Lead

To execute great design work, deep empathy is necessary. OI Coaches must create a leadership style that enhances empathy and gives it the space it needs to do its work when helping OI Innovators design radical new ways of working.

1.3 DESIGN: Transform

Design-thinking, a human-centered design approach, is probably the best way to execute the design function when coaching OI. Transcend the ego and empathize, strategize, then transition to design-thinking.

1.4 DESIGN: Coach

Coaching is incredibly empowering for people that have a growth mindset and welcome coaching. A critical aspect of coaching is to seek permission to coach first, from either the team or individual. Guiding innovators to succeed driven by their strategy while keeping them aligned to the latest developments in the organization's strategy will help them keep their innovation's design relevant.

2. TRANSFORM

2.1 TRANSFORM: Strategize

Transforming an idea into reality well is exceptionally challenging. Transforming involves business actions and managing the impacts of those actions. Mapping the transformation team's strengths and weaknesses against what needs to be done will help guide the team in effectively executing the transformation activities.

2.2 TRANSFORM: Lead

Leading transformation requires an excellent understanding of the organizational context, agendas of key stakeholders, executive processes, and so on, thus thinking ahead in terms of predicting risks and issues. The OI Innovator has to be deeply empathic when introducing radical new ways of working.

2.3 TRANSFORM: Transform

This nexus of transformation activities and transformation coaching is the much needed 'turbo boost' because executing disruption is tough! With a clear list of the business actions, it's time get business involved and get the innovation ready, also to be super-focussed on managing impacts.

2.4 TRANSFORM: Coach

With data about how successful the transformation was, once executed, it's good to unpack the lessons. Where ten employees used the OI, did they use it effectively? That data is useful in providing clues about how to repeat that Scale Plan for the next 100 employees.

3. SCALE

3.1 SCALE: Strategize

The SCALE Plans detail how to SCALE the innovation across the identified employee user groups that might use the OI. Mapping and delivering the OI against the employee's strategic needs, we then prepare the targeted employees for adopting the OI.

3.2 SCALE: Lead

Finding meaningful engagement with key-stakeholders, playing back their needs, as identified in the DESIGN phase, and demonstrating simple, highly usable and easily adoptable solutions to those needs, are critical in rolling out an OI in their space.

3.3 SCALE: Transform

Transcend to a mindset of empathy where you can lead with the other's need. Introduce the product in such a way as to alleviate sufficiently the chance of people's fear of the new, while leveraging their curiosity of the new.

3.4 SCALE: Coach

With data about how successful the SCALE Plan or Plans were, once executed, it's good to unpack the lessons.

In conclusion, OI Coaches could be the step-change in evolution from traditional management. OI Coaches would use principles and practices familiar to them as managers, such as strategizing, leadership, transformation, and coaching. As this is such a new field, we encourage the development of a global leadership team to help develop standards and content for this field.

More about this at www.InnovationCoaching.org.

19

A SILICON VALLEY MINDSET

For those with the right mindset, data that shows a path to success can be truly exciting. And if you're looking to get a large enterprise to think differently, then keep reading. The rest of this book is dedicated to helping enterprises think and work like a Silicon Valley startup, no matter their size.

By bringing together employees with the OI Mindset and focusing on opportunity data (identifying problems or value opportunities within the organization), applying the principles and practices outlined in this book, and creating an OI Culture, companies can achieve real success. Just look at the icons of Silicon Valley!

To create an OI Community within a larger organization, it's important to work with the 2.5-15% of employees who are naturally occurring innovators and early adopters, across multiple business functions. By profiling these individuals through surveys and interviews, inviting them to join an OI community with clear goals and opportunity data, and creating OI Teams that can work efficiently across functions, companies can bring their OI to life. And the more diverse the backgrounds of OI Team members, the better the design - a fundamental principle of Design Thinking, as espoused by David Kelley.

Furthermore, OI can happen anywhere within an organization, improving business areas like policies, systems, processes, and products or services. And while products like Google and Facebook are often associated with Silicon Valley, the greatest value we can derive from this innovative region is in the way they work as organizations. That's what this book is all about - helping companies adopt a Silicon Valley mindset to achieve real success. But first, business leaders must be willing and ready to let go the legacy mindset developed and not much changed, since the industrial revolution. Only then can the real AI transformation journey begin, and with a solid commitment to responsibly offsetting any negative impacts on society and the impacted workforce.

**Consider doing
the OI course on Udemy**
https://www.udemy.com/course/organizationalinnovation

(Easy access via your personal profile on InnovationCoaching.org)

Part Two

Coach OI

20

AESOP HAD THE RIGHT IDEA

In organizations, conflicts, and disagreements often arise concerning ownership and responsibility, especially so for ownership of innovation. Aesop's fable about the old farmer and his bundle of sticks provides a valuable lesson for organizations wanting to do real OI. In this 'Aesop's Fable', the farmer presented his children with a bundle of sticks tied up with a rope and challenged them to break it to claim ownership of the farm. Despite their efforts, none of them could break the bundle. The farmer then untied the bundle and gave each of his children a stick to break, which they did with ease.

This fable supports the underlying principle of OI, which is that no single person or department can 'own' or 'do' the innovation.

In OI, everyone has ownership, and the chances of success increase tremendously.

OI Coaches should contemplate this fable and think about the wisdom of the farmer's approach. Similarly, executives should understand that involving many employees in OI is better than giving a single department the job of doing OI.

OI should be done in all parts of an organization by anyone willing to be involved.

As we continue in this book, we will uncover a simple, tried, and tested practical approach, born in Silicon Valley, to coach OI for organizations of any type, anywhere in the world. Aesop had the right idea, and we can all learn from his fable to achieve success in innovation.

21

COACHING ORGANIZATIONAL INNOVATION

Coaching organizational innovation (OI) has become a crucial factor in achieving success. OI is about evolving management thinking from traditional functions to more strategic and transformative ones. The success of OI depends on the organization's appetite for finding and implementing radical new ways of doing business.

Coaching OI involves identifying and supporting potential OI innovators in the organization. It starts with training department managers to coach OI and introducing a set of processes. The initial OI coaches facilitate the success journey process with all managers, resulting in a natural eagerness to develop OI capabilities within their teams. However, for managers who find it challenging to innovate, other mechanisms such as defining an OI key performance indicator measure could be implemented.

The OI value chain is leveraged within the team to guide the team, constantly reminding them of their strengths and weaknesses and how these map to their opportunities and threats. OI can happen at all levels of the organization with varying degrees of impact value, solving problems with radical new ways of working. For OI's to be effective, they begin at a strategic level.

Organizational change, which is not innovation-driven, is changing for change-sake. Therefore, we suggest using OI to name the capabilities and resources to improve how business works. It can be implemented in organizations by an OD team but not run by it. That is the responsibility of the organization's leaders.

Leadership is a key enabler of OI. The most senior available executive must lead and manage the implementation and activation of OI within their business. Developing methods and tools such as an OI platform for management to manage strategic innovations makes it easier to track benefit realization linked to strategic objectives, rolling up into a neat 'OI to strategy' tracking dashboard. This enables the executives to see which innovations are enabling which drivers of growth. Our innovation platform, icntr, enables this and many associated data points giving executives and managers tooling to manage growth dependencies.

In conclusion, coaching OI can be thought of as the new business project management. It is a way to empower employees to become innovators with clear value data of how they are contributing to strategy. By implementing OI, employees can create levers for personal, team and business success, enhancing the organization's strategic capabilities and performance.

22

LEADING A HUMAN INNOVATION PLATFORM

Proper management of human innovation capital is crucial for the success of any organization. Failure to do so can result in adverse effects on critical business performance areas such as finance, credibility with customers, and other stakeholders. This has been demonstrated time and time again in numerous business cases. Therefore, it is essential to understand the organization's policies, culture, architecture, or business framework to introduce a human innovation platform within the organization. The stability of the core business processes is vital while innovations go through the OI Value Chain and become a new way of working, in whichever area the targeted problem existed. The human innovation platform leaders take accountability for ensuring that there is no risk to core business processes, as innovations scale.

The convergence point or the 'value-add' equilibrium, where market demand is met with intelligent supply, is the value that the organization creates. The constructs of any organization, such as people, processes, and systems, must converge in an optimal arrangement to produce the optimal 'value-add' equilibrium. People, processes, and systems must work together to achieve value for stakeholders and shareholders alike. In today's world, businesses can broaden the periphery of optimal equilibrium by responding to a wider range of challenges, quicker, with rapidly deployable employee-led innovations on the SAP S/4HANA platform, or Salesforce cloud, as examples. Therefore, managing OI around a multi-channel, multi-stakeholder, multi-system environment requires a specific type of business leader with a specific skill-set supporting executives who lead the human innovation platform and enable the OI Value Chain.

The human innovation platform owner, preferably the CEO, secures the foundation of the organization, the core, while providing the arena to do OI, aiming to expand the capabilities of the core, and its digital platform. These human innovation platform owners and co-owners, need to think more across the business instead of within the silos of the business. The age-old departmental or silo view is still very prevalent in modern business. The future is more likely, if you look at Silicon Valley organizations, going to be strategically integrated mission-critical OI teams, and the departments replaced by AI-enabled apps.

The effective convergence of systems, processes, and people relies heavily on these three principles working in balance. Leadership of OIs within an organization must be singular in its objectives and direction, otherwise this balance may become an unmanageable chaotic situation. Corporate-wide OIs must be led by the person holding the most senior position in a company because the value-chain of an organization covers the whole spectrum of its business and is fully integrated into cross-department/functionality of modern systems.

In conclusion, senior executives must take active responsibility for the implementation and activitation of OI as a new framework that will help design, transform and scale radically better ways of working, using AI and other maturing technologies. While the use of people with an intimate knowledge of coaching organizations through change is encouraged, the busines leader might familiarize themselves with the pitfalls of delegating ownership of OI. An individual OI failure can result in irreparable or costly repercussions. Therefore, a human innovation platform is critical in assisting to implement OI through OI Coaches, frameworks and a digital OI platform like icntr. To achieve success, executives must always know how much progress their teams are making using OI and data about growth as a result of successful OIs. This is why we built icntr, as a system of records and analysis for all innovations, and their respective contribution to growth.

23
THE SIGNIFICANCE OF LEADERSHIP IN DRIVING INNOVATION

Leadership plays a crucial role in driving innovation and promoting positive social contribution while attracting shareholder value. However, authentic leadership is not associated with greed, power, or domination. Instead, it it appears to be centered around how a person is perceived by others, fostering care and growth. Studies have shown that a leader who is genuinely caring and encourages growth in their team members earn legitimate leadership status. The intent of such leaders must be consistent and genuine.

In psychology, various communication and attitude models suggest that the listener subconsciously attempts to deduce the communicator's intent. In a typical work environment where the manager lacks legitimate leadership qualities, subordinates will perceive this person's communication as a means of getting other to help meet his or her objectives. This lack of leadership results in subordinates doing the bare minimum to avoid getting fired, creating an environment where innovation cannot thrive.

Legitimate leadership is in short supply in businesses, organizations, and non-profits. Teams who work under authentic leaders conduct their affairs with diligence and willingness because they are intrinsically motivated to do so. Authentic leaders foster a culture of creative problem-solving and innovation. Effective leadership is essential, not only for innovation but also for other organizational aspects such as compliance, ethics, and mitigating conflicts of interest.

The key difference between a manager and a leader is the intent. While a manager's intent is to meet planned objectives and retain their job, a leader's intent is to care for their people, build competencies, and facilitate growth, creating a community focused on the same objective - growth through innovation. This is the core principle of Deloitte's Human Centered Leadership model.

Changing an organization's culture to expect innovation and mind shifts without legitimate leadership is a recipe for failure. Innovation requires more significant effort and commitment than day-to-day operations, making legitimate leadership a crucial consideration for success.

During times of problem-solving and innovation, people need leaders who genuinely care, are transparent, and provide 'whole truths' about the mission and objectives. Creative problem-solving thrives in an innovation framework where employees feel well-taken care of. The OI leader must inspire and motivate people to keep the team's momentum alive and responsive to the needs and Success Journeys of others.

Stodgy managers result in minimal innovation, yet innovation is a key growth factor, ever more so with AI. Businesses need people who are hungry to solve problems, as growth leaders, in leadership positions. Implementing and activating OI can make an organization truly innovative. Once active, this OI framework will provide comprehensible, logical value processes relative to strategic drivers, enabling business leaders to boldly drive innovation, knowing that the frameworks and OI systems will provide the levers necessary for scaling innovation capabilities.

24

THE IMPORTANCE OF HUMAN PSYCHE IN ORGANIZATIONAL INNOVATION

In order to understand the difference between effective and ineffective OI capabilities, it is crucial to appreciate the link between the human psyche and innovation. Companies that fail to treat their employees as anything more than mere "human resources" are increasingly viewed as negative contributors to society and are less likely to survive. It has become apparent that a more holistic view of people is required in order to attract and retain the best talent, and improving brand value through the employee experience. The customer experience of a brand will only be as good as the employee's experience of the brand.

Employees are more motivated and energized when treated as individuals rather than just resources. Managers with an innovative psyche, working with employees who share this mindset, can accomplish great things. Accepting this principle is the first step toward implementing and activating real OI. Management is responsible for the psyche of their subordinates in the workplace, as well as ensuring that stakeholders have positive experiences when dealing with the organization.

Creative energy is critical for successful OI and is found within the innovative psyche, which is why it is essential to manage the collective psyche of employees with the right intent while creating a safe environment to innovate. It is possible to get the best out of people without being malicious. A controlled or disrespected employee is unlikely to innovate, while an inspired employee given the opportunity to unleash their potential in a problem situation can be just the kind of "We can do this..." psyche needed for innovations that require creative and committed energy from the workforce. This is where OI coaches come into play.

The key to unleashing a company's growth potential is OI, an exciting prospect indeed. Through the process of OI, it is often surprising to witness the people who become OI innovators. Employees across departments, from finance and maintenance to security and workshop personnel, have a vast amount of innovative enthusiasm waiting for an opportunity to become an OI innovator, making up about 2.5 to 15% of employees. We are not all born with equal logical, intellectual, or academic aptitude, and the same for innovation enthusiasm, not everyone has it. Many of us may be willing to participate in problem-solving situations, but the successful implementation of a solution requires significant effort.

Innovation is not a full-time job, but rather a full-time attitude. There is a saying that goes, "Some people make things happen, others watch things happen, and the rest wonder what happened." The future belongs to those who make things happen strategically. Kaplan and Norton wrote excellent books on how to achieve a strategy-focused organization, emphasizing that all employees should be part of the strategic dialogue. However, top management often isolates themselves, drafting strategic objectives and plans using top management terminology, and then expects the rest of the organization to buy into and achieve the goals without being part of the process. To achieve a strategy-focused organizational community, people must be brought into the strategic process, starting with mission and vision, and their psyche aligned with the organization's goals. This can only be achieved through a well-intentioned, properly structured strategy, and team performance framework.

While the psyche side of OI may seem too "fuzzy" for some, empathy is an absolute requirement for success in OI. Understanding what employees need at the deepest level is crucial in creating a more OI-active organization. For organizations that only focus on the bottom-line, disregarding their employees altogether, they may do quite well, but the success of unethical sweatshops is not a model to follow. As organizations face increasing pressure to focus on and report non-financial aspects and human-related factors, such as diversity, they must continually improve the way they do business, improving the employee experience using for example Deloitte's Human Centered leadership approach.

Another practical reason for understanding people's feelings is that they can be "signals" that help manage certain risks and issues. By being in tune with employees' feelings, organizations have the ability to build risk profiles and manage risk, thanks to clear signals from employees. However, an environment of credibility must exist where feelings are being expressed. Where OI coaches are not trusted or nonchalant towards people's feelings, they will never hear the truth until it is too late. Ignoring feelings will result in a lack of commitment, as people are no longer motivated solely by being paid. People want to do their best, but they will only give more than the bare minimum if they really want to. They need to be intrinsically motivated to do so.

Understanding people's feelings and perceptions is the foundation of successful innovations and agility to implement them. Anyone can begin the process of growth by looking at their own emotional and relational intelligence and acknowledging their shortcomings. This process can lead to a deeper understanding of one's own values and potential to make the world a better place. Maslow's later work explains that the capstone of a person's life is "Self-transcendence," which is where true psychology (the meaning of the soul as a translation from latin) can be understood. Therefore, to change the world, we must start with ourselves. It would be wonderful if management schools taught the hierarchy of needs to achieve self-transcendence, and not just self-realisation, which is the outdated version we see in business schools.

25

THE ROLE OF MANAGERS IN MODERN ORGANIZATIONS

The history of modern management has been a journey of evolution and change. From the forward-thinking industrialist Robert Owens, who offered his employees comfortable housing and training opportunities, to the American concept of Scientific Management and the European concept of Classical Management, the aim has always been to use people to achieve shareholder wealth. However, while classical management viewed people as mere functions in an organized system, the American scientific school realized that treating workers well led to better productivity. The Human Relations view, which emphasized the importance of social frameworks in corporate communities, highlighted the need to reduce the psychological and productivity impacts of Organizational Change, leading to the rise of Organizational Change Management interventions and programs.

Leading a human-centric organization through change requires sincere, credible leaders who have a deep passion for caring and growing people. Transparency and mutual respect between leaders and informal leaders are key to building trust and achieving success. Educating the workforce is also crucial to preventing group-think scenarios among people not familiar with critical business principles, sharing only fears or concerns.

The Organizational Change Management process has three phases: the known present, the transition, and the desired outcome. The transition phase is the most painful and requires careful planning and execution to achieve the desired outcome. While technological innovations have received much attention and investment, the development of managers into real OI Coaches has been neglected. OI Coaches can help improve cross-functional systems, processes, and people collaboration, leading to successful implementation and activation of OI, through contributing to developing the organisation's human innovation platform.

HR Departments have been responsible for improving innovation capabilities but lack the budget and authority to do so effectively. Implementing and activating OI needs to be a CEO-led initiative, with HR making recommendations for training and developing OI Coaches. A corporate-wide OI policy and strategy can be introduced, along with a digital platform to enable the success of the OI Coaches. Coaching OI should become a daily function of all people in management and leadership positions.

Managers need to understand cross-functional processes, systems, and how to coach, to become successful in modern organizations. They should also consider the Liberal Art side of leadership, such as caring for employees and supporting their Success Journeys. Modern management has social and environmental responsibilities and is expected to lead with a vision for a sustainably growing organization that makes a positive contribution to society. Technical people should be adequately rewarded rather than promoted to management positions to retain their talent. Too often we see technically brilliant people made into managers, in order to meet their salary and growth desires, but without proper management and leadership training, they are only going to be terrible managers.

In conclusion, good managers who can work effectively with technical people are essential for organizations to take advantage of the growth opportunities of the new economies that the fourth industrial revolution is bringing. The role of managers has evolved from controlling and influencing people, to caring for and growing them, leading to successful innovations and a sustainable future. Managers, trained and empowered to coach OI, are key to getting organisations ready for the AI future.

26

ORGANIZATIONAL INNOVATION AND CORPORATE CULTURE

Implementing and activating OI capabilities is not just about implementing new ways of working, it's also about changing the existing cultural structure of the organization. To successfully introduce OI capabilities, it's essential to understand the current corporate culture and leverage its dynamics to build OI capabilities. However, it's equally important to identify potential risks and barriers that may be lurking beneath the surface of day-to-day operations and employee stability. When implemented with the right intentions, OI can turn potential people barriers into enablers of change.

To use organisational culture as an enabler, there are three key constructs that an OI leader must gather information on and incorporate into the OI process data. These are: leaders, stories, and rituals.

Identifying official and unofficial leaders is essential, as these individuals can have a significant influence on the organization's culture. People in positions of power can also become great OI coaches. Understanding the stories that circulate through official and unofficial channels can provide insight into the organizational psyche and past experiences with transformations, as in, they were either good or bad. Identifying stories that foster a healthy sentiment can also help build a culture more focused on successful OI.

Rituals, such as celebratory lunches and management forums, can be used to promote consistent change messages and obtain support for OI processes. By leveraging these three constructs, OI Leaders can build a culture that is more conducive to successful OI.

27

OI AND CORPORATE GOVERNANCE

The business world was rocked by the governance disasters of Enron and WorldCom, leading to the implementation of a new governance framework in the United States that we know as Sarbanes-Oxley (SoX). This framework was based on penalizing non-compliance, with a strict "comply or else" mentality. However, it was widely acknowledged that this approach did not achieve the desired results.

Other countries had previously implemented similar frameworks, but with a more lenient "comply or explain" principle. Under this principle, non-compliance could be excused if a reasonable explanation was provided. Regardless of the approach, publicly listed companies around the world were required to have some form of risk management processes in place to govern compliance risk.

Business risk resulting from projects can be substantial, as demonstrated by the well-known example of HP. A new system implementation caused serious order backlogs and lost revenue. Implementing OI processes and systems is simply good governance, as they provide the guard rails, records and workflows to make OI easier and increase the chance of success.

For a company to fly the flag of good corporate governance, it should have proper OI governance and processes in place, primarily because it will require people and capital to be successful. Good governance and compliance can serve the organizations agenda and safeguard against short-terminism and other risks like ignoring the innovation agenda, making effective good governance an essential part of any successful business strategy. Especially true for implementing and activating OI capabilities, ensuring that well articulated problem definitions are the root of an innovation.

28

THE IMPORTANCE OF THE OI SCHEDULE IN PRIORITIZING INNOVATIONS

In any organization, various OIs can occur simultaneously, some of which do not even come to the notice of senior management. However, it is crucial to have an OI Schedule that lists all the OIs and prioritizes them based on their impact on the organization's success. This can be done using the digital OI platform, which can help employees better understand the importance and priority of each OI requirement and its associated actions and impacts.

It's important to get the OI schedule right, as there may need to be careful coordination where innovations are integrated or impact other aspects of the business. This means the involvement of senior management as OI quality gate controllers to assess the impact of each OI on the organization's operating core. By identifying the stakeholders who will be impacted and the effect on them, it is possible to manage the risk of too many changes happening at the same time, resulting in confusion and operational chaos.

Strategic objectives that are used in the OI Design Feasibility Study are key in terms of prioritizing OIs. The Time Quadrant by Stephen Covey can assist in understanding how to arrange conflicting priorities and determine what is important versus what is urgent. Involving key stakeholders in the assessment process can foster strategic conversations among the executive ranks, leading to the identification of more impacts that need to be considered and attached to the OI TRANSFORM or SCALE data records.

True leaders take accountability for their organization's strategic direction and achievement. This means involving all key stakeholders in the business case to avoid making regrettable decisions, as seen in the case of the AOL acquisition by Time Warner. Once the strategic objectives are understood and stakeholders buy into them, it becomes easier to implement OI Business Actions because people understand why changes have to happen, serving as the guiding mission and vision for the organization's purpose and game plan.

29

OI PRINCIPLES FOR SUCCESSFUL TRANSFORMATION

Transformation is a crucial aspect of OI and involves the efforts of many people. Managing transformation can be broken down into two strategies: Transcendence and Transition. The Transcendence strategy involves a mind-shift in values, culture, and leadership, while the Transition strategy focuses on changes in the business processes, policies, and jobs. Integrating these two strategies is essential to achieve a successful OI Transformation.

To achieve Transcendence, organizations must leverage their culture's constructs, such as Leadership, Stories, and Rituals. Organizational Development experts are instrumental in developing and executing strategies to achieve transcendence, which is a critical aspect of an organization's OI journey.

Transition requires detailed analysis and management of all impacted tangibles and intangibles in an organization, such as digital systems, processes, and job procedures. Business risk response plans can be used to prepare for the go-live of an innovation, completing these plans is one of the activities, part of the Business Actions required for the OI TRANSFORM step.

Combining the Transcendence and Transition strategies during the OI TRANSFORM "Business Action" is critical for success. All OI Transition activities must work the desired transcendence values into the activities while giving people reasons for doing things in a well-communicated strategic context. OI Leaders must introduce the new with the familiar by up-skilling employees with OI Innovation and Coaching practices, instead of the old-style command and control leadership, which creates a barrier to creativity, thus blocking OI.

Emerging markets have gone through incredible transformation in their fledgling years as new democracies and innovations focused on GDP growth. However, the transition process from old to new generally has been weak, leaving the country vulnerable to corruption and open to people and foreign powers with wayward and devious agendas. Any transformation coupled with well-planned and executed Transcendence and Transition strategies has a better chance of sustainable success.

The five OI Principles are crucial for successful OI capability building. They are:

> 1. Coaching OI,
> 2. Success Journeys of Employees,
> 3. DESIGN,
> 4. TRANSFORM,
> 5. SCALE.

Managers should be trained on these principles and be included in their performance indicators. Managers should also help employees understand that they can change the world or at least the organization they work in, explaining the OI Value Chain and how employees can use it to solve problems in the work place.

30
PRINCIPLE 1: COACHING OI

In order to achieve optimal results in coaching OI within an organization, it is crucial for training people to become OI Coaches to be owned and driven by the executive body. This involves senior management making decisions about the mission and vision for their organization's innovation ambitions, and how that drives Coaching OI, and OI enterprise digital capabilities and processes, as outlined in an OI policy. These aspects can be defined to be constructs of the organisation's Human Innovation Platform (HIP).

Thinking of this HIP as a franchise can be a helpful metaphor for understanding what ownership of HIP and its principles like coaching OI, entails. The HIP, once setup in the OI digital platform to enable OI Processes across the organization, contains the HIP operating guide which every team can use in to design, transform and scale radically better ways of working. HIP Leaders can then promote the HIP services to their teams and stakeholders, becoming innovation service providers, as OI coaches for their teams and stakeholders. This ensures everyone is on the same page regarding the impacts of innovation, increasing efficiency and reducing risks of negative disruption.

Additionally, an organization can 'franchise' their OI Capabilities to the multi-stakeholder eco-system they are a part of, such as the supply-chain or customers trying to solve problems themselves. This will become necessary as we try to solve complex climate related issues across industries.

Through an OI policy, senior management can commit to supporting and enabling managers as OI Coaches to lead OI within their department as HIP franchise owners, ultimately accountable for successful OI. Just like McDonalds is the franchise and a burger is the output, the HIP is the franchise and the innovation is the output. This HIP franchise model can emphasize OI Ownership by all management, thereby building the right culture through the OI Value Chain and respective multi-stakeholder eco-system, with HIPs all over.

It is important for senior management to take ownership of the value from all the HIPs across the business. OI Processes drive growth and are required for continued organizational success in the brave new world of AI, where at least half of AI use-cases don't come from the IT team, but from the people doing the job. All executives are accountable for growth, which mainly comes from innovation. Therefore, successfully leading the HIP may be a performance metric, against which executives may held to account by shareholders and other key stakeholders if the organization fails to achieve its goals. This is why ownership of OI should never be fully delegated, and top management must assume ownership of the HIP delivering OI value, as a practice throughout the organization. To learn more about the steps for getting senior management to setup a HIP, refer to the TRANSFORMATION parts of this book in the context of the OI Value Chain. With proper ownership and coaching of OI, organizations can achieve greater success in their innovation and growth efforts.

31

PRINCIPLE 2: SUCCESS JOURNEYS

As we've discussed earlier in this book, Success Journeys of the employees are a crucial aspect of achieving success in business where the potential of AI will be realised mostly by the people doing the work. Managing employees and the stakeholder groups they work in, during multiple innovations in the process of designing, transforming and scaling radically better ways of working, can be a complex and challenging task. That's where the digital OI platform icntr, at InnovationCoaching.org can be super useful.

The icntr cloud platform is a set of databases that functions as a 'System of Records' for data related to OIs. It enables collaboration, process, governance, workflows, reporting, compliance, and risk management where the innovation impacts stakeholder groups.

The first step in the OI Value Chain is to identify stakeholder groups to work with and use the Success Journey approach, identifying their mission, vision, strategies, and associated strategic objectives, co-exploring challenges they may be having. The OI Platform is used to gather all the data collected from stakeholder groups. This ensures that all stakeholder groups are included in the process and that no stakeholders are left out of the impact analysis and work done to align them to the new way of working.

But it's not just about identifying stakeholder groups. It's also about managing them effectively. icntr Has a stakeholder analysis process where a database of these stakeholder groups is maintained in a system against categories like Organizational Scope, Internal Direct, Internal Indirect, External Direct, and External Indirect.

Once the stakeholder groups have been identified, the next step is to identify key stakeholders. These are the people who will represent or be a channel of communication for a stakeholder group. Again, icntr helps to manage these OI processes, working with such key stakeholders and their respective OI Coaches across the organization.

It's perhaps critical to consider the influence key stakeholders could have on the innovation and the degree to which they need to be involved in mind-shift exercises. This is where the stakeholder analysis comes in handy. It helps to identify stakeholders who require absolute stability of service or product supply as the innovation is implemented. It also identifies stakeholders who are initially supportive of the OI and respective organizational changes and are willing to be 'understanding' of the organization's expected operational instability resulting in temporary poor service levels. On the other hand, it also identifies stakeholders who will be affected in a net-negative way vs. those who are likely to benefit from the innovation. Here, icntr makes it easier to slice and dice the numbers into the various categories of stakeholder groups and required involvement for alignment to the new way of business. This is to understand the effort required and enable the organization to manage the stakeholder engagement process in a quantifiable manner.

In conclusion, managing stakeholder groups is crucial for the success of any organization. Using a system like icntr can help organizations manage stakeholders effectively and efficiently, ensuring that all stakeholder groups are included in the process and that no key stakeholders are left out.

32

PRINCIPLE 3: DESIGN

Continuous growth in business requires constant management of capital, identified as Capital Expenditure or simply CAPEX. When additional capital is required, capital is sought from outside of the business. However, this is never free, and for businesses, it means competing in the market for capital, appeasing whoever will lend capital, with whatever their appetite is for interest and risk. Either way, capital is utilised internally with interest known as Internal Rate of Return (IRR). This is an accounting definition for the rate of interest charged for the use of capital in an organization. This rate is essential for innovators to incorporate into their feasibility calculations when determining the return on their innovation investment.

The optimal use of capital is a culture that has been emphasized by business leaders such as Steve Jobs in both Apple and his lesser-known venture, NEXT Computers. Nickel-and-diming should be the way things get procured not only for "early days" startups but also for large organizations. This is especially true fro getting innovations started and scaled.

Formulating business cases may seem irksome to most managers, but for those coached in OI, it is a way to test the ground-up demand for the OI and the true costs of the transformation and scale steps in the OI Value Chain. Two perspectives for business cases, top-down and bottom-up, are used in OI DESIGN feasibility studies, with a focus on financials.

The top-down feasibility is based on high-level assumptions and arrives at figures using broad-based numbers, whether the problem the innovation will fix is in the domain of an internal stakeholder group or an external market segment. The bottom-up feasibility details the initial investment required in the OI and the cost to transform the OI from idea to reality, whether that be a small OI within the business or the introduction of an electric vehicle to the mass market. It will also detail the unit economics where, for external customers, it may be real currency value or for internal customers where the measure may be in savings.

Managing the business case with a calibrated top-down/

bottom-up view integrated with the execution processes ensures that the initial expectations of the innovation are kept under control. OI processes work well when they provide dynamic updates to the business case in its ROI measurement. The importance of design in OI cannot be overstated as it is essential to have a well-planned and executed feasibility study to ensure the success of the innovation investment.

33

PRINCIPLE 4: TRANSFORM

Thanks to AI's disruption on the business world, traditional project management principles may fall short when it comes to achieving resilience and getting ahead with AI. While these principles work well for building physical assets like houses, they fail to account for the unique challenges posed by AI innovations. For instance, an AI solution which matches an employee's capabilities to an internal gig-board, if project managed, may focus on building the AI, but neglect to consider how to manage for example the impact on the career aspirations of people the gigs may have.

Organizational Change Management (OCM) is often added to project management principles to address business impacts. However, this approach can be ineffective, as a Business Impact Analysis or BIA, is often too high-level, and OCM managers can only possibly know some aspects of detailed business procedures and systems. This can lead to confusion and challenges during project go-lives. The solution? The TRANSFORM step in the OI Value Chain.

By integrating Transcendence and Transition strategies, businesses can approach transformation more effectively. This balanced approach involves sequencing actions and identifying the resulting impact and its respective risk response. For example, when breaking down a wall in a house, it's vital to assess the load on top of that wall and insert a support beam before knocking it down. This is likely a single action on the project plan, 'Knock hole in wall'. Only builders knowledgable in how to mitigate the risk of this action, will prevent the wall collapsing.

The OI Value Chain provides a framework for integrating this transformational approach into innovation processes. It's not a standalone "ivory tower" approach but an integrated part of the overall OI process. By training OI Coaches, businesses can successfully navigate the complexities of micro-transformations and ensure innovation success.

To achieve a successful innovation-led transformation, it is vital to adopt a balanced approach. This means planning and executing actions and impacts as one, and identifying and addressing the risks associated with each action. By following this approach, businesses can ensure that their transformational efforts are successful and that they achieve their desired outcomes with the innovation.

At the heart of this approach is the TRANSFORM step in the OI Value Chain. By integrating this step into their overall process, businesses can effectively navigate the complexities of transformation and ensure project success. This approach is not a standalone solution, but rather an integrated part of the overall process, and by training OI Coaches, businesses can ensure that they have the skills and knowledge necessary to achieve successful innovations.

34

PRINCIPLE 5: SCALE

Scaling the innovation is a critical component of effective OI. Benefits realization is often used to measure and improve the business case ROI of projects, but it does not always identify the readiness of users or employees, nor plan tasks to improve innovation buy-in and adoption by stakeholders. This is where benefits are identified and realized as part of the SCALE step.

The SME of a particular business process, for example, accounts-receivable, is the person who re-engineers the 'to-be' desired state for their process and can make a great OI Innovator. This person normally has seniority and experience on their side and has been given the authority to design the best way of doing business and is expected to continually innovate, in a consultative process with respective business stakeholders. This probably doesn't happen in reality. This is why we need OI.

In this SCALE step we prioritize the impact in terms of how it will affect which stakeholder groups and also understand the risk to the OI if the impacted stakeholders may not have been fully prepared in time for the activation of the innovation or the Business Actions. In order to prepare stakeholder groups for the OI, communications, education, and training are key to ensuring innovation value can deliver as planned. In the case of OI, SCALE Plans are planned and rolled-out into specified stakeholder groups.

Regarding business alignment, a practical warehouse management OI scenario is the re-numbering of storage bins and locations in a warehouse because of a new app related innovation, enabling standardization across the organization of storage locations.

This is an impact that may require senior management leadership.

The process for registering OI Value Chain SCALE impacts is as follows:

Step 1: Create awareness of the innovation and the impacts on activities related to storage locations in warehouses, amongst the impacted stakeholder groups.

Step 2: Hold further workshops with a balance of senior business people and the doers, i.e. people who actually do the job related to warehouse storage locations.

Step 3: Once the new way is presented as a diagrammatical process, and in steps, to the same group of people, facilitate a session whereby people provide their insights as to what may have to be changed in order to do business with the proposed innovation.

Education and training in scaling the proposed innovation is important for enabling people to be able to adequately carry out the responsibilities of the process roles that they have been given in the new way of doing business. In many cases of innovation, there are new things that will have to be understood. It may be, for example, education about new purchasing policies and/or new system training.

Whatever the new requirement is of the employee, learning will be key to the employees adaption to the new way of doing business. Often, training executed within a tight budget is not enough to prepare people. For this reason, it is important to look past the immediate perceived training requirement and understand that successful organizations endeavor to be learning organizations.

The SCALE process to use while creating documentation for this step could be structured and signed-off in the sequence as follows: SCALE Charter, SCALE Strategy, SCALE Plan, Learning Curriculums, Training Event Schedules, Evaluations, Reports, Templates, Working Document Repository, Audit Trail.

Creating a learning organization is vital to the success of OI as it enables people to carry out their responsibilities effectively and efficiently in the new way of doing business. Education and training are key components of the process, and the SCALE process provides a structured approach to manage these activities effectively.

Part Three

Implementing OI

35

THE OI DESIRED STATE

The OI Value Chain needs to be be adequately managed using a robust framework that consists of planning, budgeting, resource-management, tasks, time-frames, progress-reporting and mitigation of risks and issues, for the OI Value Chain to effectively support the innovations.

This might sound like a project, but it's not. The reason is that a project works with a Project Management Office, or PMO mindset, owning delivery. In OI, the departments own innovation delivery. What is required for managing OI, are the application of the coaching functions we introduced earlier in this book (Strategize, Lead, Transform and Coach) within the OI Value Chain positioned around the core of the business, directly integrating with the core of the business. The OI Value Chain processes when positioned around the business core, can more easily integrate with the finance processes which run through every facet of the organization, ensuring robust and dynamic feasibility management of an innovation. Also, a PMO manages a single large scope of work per project, not lots of small scopes of work which is done to get many different innovations working.

Unfortunately many well-meaning and potentially valuable innovation initiatives are setup as projects, and launched but not managed as an integrated component of business. Then, because it's managed from a distant ivory tower, it misses the essence of the problem, and the solution is more of a pain than it is a gain, leaving yet another potential world-changing innovation, dead. The old adage 'what's worth doing, is worth doing well' is very applicable, especially when dealing with a situation where an organization, its shareholders and other stakeholder's livelihood, is at stake.

As we go through the remainder of this book, it would be worthwhile to try and understand how the principles of OI, as mentioned in the previous chapters, can be managed by every single line manager and those handfuls of employees that seem to make everything happen. The natural innovators (2.5-15% of managers and employees) will want to own and execute the processes of OI in an organization, to bring those innovations to reality, not a project management office, who will likely think of it as another day in the office. Project Management and a PMO is great if you're executing a civil engineering project, but terrible for innovation and business ownership. The remainder of this book will provide guidelines and tips as to how OI and HIPS can be implemented and activated.

More specifically, the next two chapters focus on the OI policies, charters and capabilities required to establish the foundations of the OI capabilities, and how to build the HIP Workstreams that will collaborate to DESIGN, TRANSFORM and SCALE radically better ways of working. These will be followed by two chapters that introduce two Key Objectives and their respective OI implementation and activation phases.

There's no surprise, that to implement OI in an organization, we suggest using the OI Value Chain. With the OI Value Chain implemented with enabling digital and human platforms, the organization can consider itself to be OI active.

36

THE IMPORTANCE OF OI POLICIES AND CHARTERS

Abraham Lincoln used to say, "Give me six hours to chop down a tree and I will spend the first four sharpening the axe." This sentiment rings true when it comes to implementing OI processes. The majority of the preparation involved revolves around the creation and documentation of OI concepts, aligning approaches amongst management levels, and signing acceptance of certain governance processes and escalation guidelines. This is achieved through the use of OI Governance Policies.

The writing of an OI policy is a collective effort that combines the shared values, concepts, and ideas of like-minded individuals for the purpose of formalizing an OI model and presenting it as a cohesive group with a brand new mission to scale OI in the organization. This is a crucial step as it sets the foundation for the organization's OI strategy moving forward. This is where the messaging, values, and personal objectives are shared, and the principles of Organizational Innovation are highlighted and agreed upon as the guiding principles of OI implementation and activation within the organization.

Some of the principles that should be focused on include: encouraging people to learn how to benefit personally from the innovation processes, building an innovative step-change in how the organization will reframe itself of growth in this age of AI, entrusting innovation activities to as many people as possible, focusing on coaching principles rather than legacy management practices, developing innovation strategies and their performance, discouraging continuous focus on urgent or knee-jerk activities, and empowering people to be driven by personal mastery, meaningful innovation contribution, and the enablement of a dynamic, thriving community. Attention to detail should also be driven, especially around innovation unit economics.

It's important to note that the OI Policy is not simply a document – it's the backbone of all OI activities. Once the OI Charter is complete, an accompanying presentation that encompasses the key points of the OI policy and charter will provide a useful summary of what the organization plans to do with OI. It's crucial that the executives of the company are educated about what is in the policy and that they understand their roles and responsibilities in the OI processes and HIPs.

There are five policies that should be developed, understood, and signed-off by the senior management who are involved. These policies include the Coaching OI policy, which focuses on OI ownership, leadership, capabilities, and the approach to the OI processes and management thereof; the Success Journey of the Employee policy, which focuses on the approach to identifying, analyzing, and managing OI stakeholders; the DESIGN policy, which determines what amount of risk and investment return is required to accept feasibility outcome; the TRANSFORM policy, which focuses on how changes to the business are going to be managed; and the SCALE policy, which focuses on the communication methods, channels, and two-way communication process with stakeholders.

When developing these policies, it's helpful if they flow from a Corporate OI Strategy. This ensures that the policies have sufficient detail to give the resulting strategies clear objectives that can be easily copied across into new OI process documents or uploaded into the digital OI platform. Once this is complete, detail activities, time-frames, and OI process roles clarification, using charters for each HIP

Workstream. It's important to keep terminology consistent throughout the communications, roles, and documentation processes. Using the same terminology throughout all OI documentation makes it easier for people who are on the periphery of the OI activities to follow and understand the themes all the way through.

As you can see, nearly all the 'Ownership' principle of OI, within the preparation part of implementing OI processes, is focused on coaching leaders to understand the processes, accept responsibility of the innovations and required changes, commit to the process, and learn how the process of personal continuous growth can be developed with OI. This education, understanding, and acceptance of leadership roles is achieved through developing the policies discussed above in conjunction with the respective leaders.

37
DESIGNING ORGANIZATIONAL INNOVATION CAPABILITIES

Organizational innovation (OI) can be successful only if key principles are understood and supported across departments and teams. Timing is crucial, and OI principles should be handled by different OI workstreams, representing every department across the organization. These workstreams work together to support the OI value chain for each innovation, depending on how it impacts stakeholder groups. OI coaches educate all OI innovators to enter innovation data onto the OI platform to effectively design, transform, and scale different innovations simultaneously. Here's some suggestions about which executive might be best positioned to lead each of the three OI workstreams. For example, the Design workstream can be led by a marketing executive. The Transform workstream could be led by an operations executive, and the Scale workstream could be led by an HR executive. These, along with the OI leading executive, constitute and report into the OI leadership team.

An OI executive workshop would be useful to prepare executives to lead their respective OI workstreams. Once executives are ready to build their workstream, they need to identify who will work with them on their respective OI workstreams. The first person who would be identified per stream is the coach or coaches for the workstream lead and they in turn can recruit internally, other workstream members.

The OI workstreams are part-time roles, where during weekly meetings innovators, innovations, progress, risks and issues are discussed, and actions or escalations are agreed. Meetings are intended to encourage cross-team collaboration and better integration of innovations, so it is essential to have a balanced team, including those who may be perceived as negative towards innovation as they are typically really good at spotting risks, and should be encouraged to call them out.

Executives ready for their role as an OI leader of their respective workstream could be trained using executive OI lead training offered by an external OI capability vendor such as ICO (InnovationCoaching.org). Once the OI workstreams have been kicked off, the organization is ready to be transformed. Every hour of OI preparation invested before the new way of doing business is switched on could save weeks of problem fixing and loads of money wasted due to confusion and lack of understanding of how to innovate across the organization using OI.

Selecting people for the OI workstreams is crucial. People considered to be risk-averse, can sometimes be valuable in balancing activities and providing a critical view of things. In small companies, there may only be three or four people per team, while larger organizations may have up to forty people per OI workstream. Getting as many people involved in OI activities as possible is highly important, given that the bulk of OI use-cases will come from people trying to solve their own problems.

Preparing executives for their innovation lead role is essential. Once the executives have signed off, accepting their role and the accountabilities that go with it, they will have esenryially agreed to setup a Human Innovation Platform using a template contracting document that can be accessed at ICO's website. This site has a wealth of information that can also be used to provide executives more clarity on their role. These OI workstreams need to be activated, and the people in the workstreams need to be educated about what they will be asked to do. ICO offers jumpstart presentations that can assist with the these kick-off sessions.

38

TRANSFORMING TO AN OI ACTIVE ORGANIZATION

In this chapter, we will explore the process of coaching OI workstreams and transforming the organization to be OI active. The success of this transformation for an organization depends on the seriousness and commitment of its stakeholders. An organization-wide kick-off event can ignite a recruitment drive to sign up employees and other stakeholders to get involved with OI as OI coaches or OI innovators, or within the OI workstreams.

OI requires managing the people-side of innovation, which is often seen as the soft side. These are generally unknown activities. However, the people-side of innovation must be led by the highest accessible executive, creating a cadence of messaging that will de-risk the probability of culture drift as a result of innovations being used to reduce headcount. If employees are asked to engage in innovation work, but they are left to assume it is to create automation that will reduce jobs and career opportunities, they might not be too happy about it. This unhappiness at scale, can cause a downward spiralling culture. Senior management, signed into their OI roles, taking ownership of the OI transformation towards becoming a more innovative organization, will drive a strategy very much required for future existence. It is necessary to get the executive mindset OI-centric and the role that they are to play, in order for OI to be successful.

The traditional executive may prefer to delegate managing the soft side of innovation to a Design Thinking specialist, or HR coach, maybe a person with soft skills fulfilling the consulting role of change management lead. However, managing and leading a human-centric approach sends a clear message to the organization, that innovation is about helping employees achieve success, not the business. So it is much more than just dealing with people's emotions and getting people excited through creative communication campaigns. It is most important that executives understand their role in transforming to an OI active organization, also being familiar with all the innovations in the pipeline. They need to be committed to supporting the mission of becoming a more innovative organization. Some innovations will rock the boat, but OI leaders are there to ensure the compass point remains and to lead and support innovations no matter how scary they may seem. Supporting and advisory partners may be there to contribute, but they should not be the ones leading the organization to become OI active.

The OI lead contracting discussion is an alignment principle that is captured in a document outlining what each party expects from the other, between executives and the respective OI trusted advisers. These agreements explicitly outline what is expected of the OI lead and the Human Innovation Platform. They then need to sign the OI commitment document and commit in spirit to OI. This is the singular most important part of the OI transformation journey and possibly the most testing for an executive, as to how they perceive the future, and their role in it.

After the OI leadership contracting is done, the OI workstream charter needs to be developed and signed off for each OI workstream (Coaching OI, Technology, DESIGN, TRANSFORM, SCALE). Stakeholder analysis needs to be done, and once the analysis is done, stakeholder management and engagement at this point is at the key-stakeholder level, merely introducing certain OI concepts to key individuals and beginning to obtain their support of the high-level view of the desired state. In the OI transform phase, before starting to do OI, all of the datasets containing stakeholder details at an individual level will have been uploaded to the OI platform. Key stakeholders could at this point be educated about their role as key-stakeholder and for which stakeholder groups they are responsible. Further education about how the communications will be channeled could also be done, thus giving them a holistic view of the 'push,' 'pull,' 'profile' communications processes, as set out in the SCALE workstream charter and its framework.

The Technology workstream will build a stakeholder group database in the OI platform, which can then be used to identify stakeholder groups agains the impact activity as part of the TRANSFORM step for each innovation. The DESIGN workstream focuses on developing design-thinking workshops around the organization, developing a design-thinking culture, related to OI.

The TRANSFORM workstream is key to successful, scalable and sustainable innovations.

The business actions and impact management is the alignment of organizational aspects to the new way of doing business, that each innovation will introduce. In the TRANSFORM part of implementing OI as a capability, only the approach (the TRANSFORM charter, signed-off) and education sessions about analyzing and mapping business impacts of implementing innovations need to be completed.

The SCALE workstream focuses on obtaining the respective 'master data' that represents the learning landscape. A mind-map of all the details that you believe will define the parameters in which the communication, education, and training processes must be executed will be helpful. As communications involve public relations work, it is critical at this point that the interactions between stakeholders and the OI workstream are looked after very well. Especially as mentioned previously, to avoid culture drift, as AI hits the headlines about affecting jobs. Anybody in a key role at this point who has negative or destructive feelings about the innovation, especially about AI, will need special attention in terms of understanding their concerns - indicating where in the innovation process those risks will be mitigated, by either retraining, or some or other supportive career progression plan.

In conclusion, the OI transformation journey requires a systematic approach, with coaching OI workstreams being a critical component. The OI lead alignment and contracting is a principle that is captured in a document outlining what each party expects from the other, between executives and the respective internal OI trusted adviser. Stakeholder analysis, stakeholder management, and engagement, and the development of a communication plan are all key components of a successfully transforming to an innovative and OI active organization.

39

SCALING OI IN YOUR ORGANIZATION

Every organization should desire to be OI active, but achieving this requires the completion of the OI transformation journey. Once the OI executives are in place as OI workstream leads, OI workstreams have been created, and the OI platform is prepared, the organization can begin scaling OI across the organization, team by team, rolling out the OI communications, education and training

Executive involvement is crucial at this point, as they have the required decision-making skills and influence with executive peers to address cross-functional decision-making, policies, procedures, and enterprise system innovations. Although the OI workstreams can continue without much executive involvement, those areas where they are required can make a difference between successful or failed OI scaling. Having executives lead teams has several advantages. One of these benefits is that it allows executives to stay informed about the latest methods of conducting business in a dynamic business landscape. Moreover, when making crucial decisions, executives possess firsthand information on the potential consequences and can better understand the innovation's context. They will also be able to prioritize innovation activities within the ranks.

The TRANSFORM workstream manages business impacts as a result of introducing the innovation, and aligns the business to the new way, collecting basic information about functional areas of business being impacted, roles, policies, processes, strategic KPIs, systems, and standard operating procedures. The impacts of implementing these OI capabilities and the organisation's Human Innovation Platform are registered against the business actions, and ownership of alignment activities is assigned to those individuals who in turn will cascade this ownership, wherever the impact is identified across the business. This can happen by them inspiring their peers to do some of the impact alignment activities, promoting the potential benefits of for example AI, to them. Also, executive messaging that innovation is mission-critical for growth, will remind people how important it is to become an OI active organization.

The SCALE workstream focuses on enabling individuals to innovate effectively across teams, with clear communications, education, and training activities for every innovation. These activities, including performance management, and accountability processes must be in place to effectively enable coaches, innovators, and impacted stakeholder groups to become more effective and innovative. Accountability processes are there to help coach. True leadership holds people accountable with the intent that the person becomes aware of their error and through a constructive feedback loop will lead them to increase their capability and capacity for innovation and rapid changes that come with it.

Communication activities throughout the OI capability implementation journey, shape and shift mindsets in a way that is aligned with OI principles and practices. Stakeholder group 'profiling' feedback influences the content of the 'push' and 'pull' communication channels. Keeping knee-jerk communications and shooting from the hip communications to a minimum is essential. It is important to plan the work, and work the plan when it comes to communications, ensuring that the key 'push/pull' communications do the job of mitigating the identified profiled risks.

In conclusion, scaling OI capabilities in your organization can be hugely rewarding for the right profile of business leader. Encouraging people to grow through attending OI sessions will also increase the leadership legitimacy of the manager, and their people will be prepared for the AI future and new ways of doing business by understanding what is expected of them in the newly formulated innovation roles. By following the principles and practices outlined in this book, organizations can improve the chances of success in building OI capabilities, leading to innovation, the primary driver of growth.

40

ACTIVATING THE HUMAN INNOVATION PLATFORM

Once the Human Innovation Platform is active, it's time to celebrate! This is a crucial moment for any organization, as it marks the successful implementation of a vision that has been in the works for some time. To commemorate this achievement, it's highly recommended to hold a final 'OI is active' session, which considers the success of the implementation journey. During this session, all related signees of the commitment to implement the vision should unanimously agree that it has been implemented.

It's important to express your gratitude to the people who contributed their time and effort to make this possible. As Aesop may have wisely added to his fable, "Don't forget to thank the people who together broke their own stick to make it happen." This gesture of appreciation goes a long way in fostering a positive culture of innovation within the organization.

As the HIP begins to activate, OI innovators should do the same by encouraging celebration and thanking the people who made it happen. It's also worth considering a financial payout promise relative to the following years added value of the HIP and all its coaches and innovators. This incentivizes further innovation and ensures that the organization continues to thrive in the long run. Think of it as a mini Silicon Valley where teams creating value, are rewarded.

Overall, activating the HIP is a significant milestone for any organization. By celebrating this achievement and expressing gratitude to those who made it happen, you lay the foundation for a culture of innovation and will have transitioned to a new set of capabilities, that will drive success for years to come.

41

ICO GLOBAL LEADERSHIP TEAM

To ensure that OI grows and thrives, the ICO Global Leadership Team (GLT) has set its sights on identifying exceptional OI coaches who will be invited to join their non-profit initiative at InnovationCoaching.Org.

These global leaders can play a vital role in the direction-setting of OI globally and assist others in building their OI advisory and coaching skills. Also offering consulting services for organisations wanting to become OI active.

For the ICO GLT to be successful and sustainable, it aims to partner with global corporations who view non-profit initiatives like ICO as key to developing innovation capabilities in industries to support the scale of step changes we're facing driving by technology advances and climate change. By building an ICO innovation ecosystem throughout the world, we can continue to push the boundaries of what is possible and create a brighter, more prosperous future for all. At ICO, we firmly believe in prioritizing humanity in innovation. This means that social responsibility is just as essential as technological advancement, as we will be encountering significant global challenges that require large-scale social innovation.

42

ICO AS A STARTUP

As one of the newest topics in the business world, OI is built on the foundation of giants such as Design Thinking, Project Management, and Organizational Change Management. At ICO, we ask for your patience and support as we continue to develop this thinking on a global scale. We strive to refine our content and tools as we move forward, and we appreciate your understanding as we work towards creating updated versions of this book and content at InnovationCoaching.org.

In the fast-paced world of Silicon Valley, it's said that if you're not embarrassed by your new product, then you're too late. As we embrace the potential of OI, anyone interested is welcome to connect with me on LinkedIn. Together, we can explore the vast potential of this topic and learn from one another.

—-

As a startup, we understand the challenges and excitement that come with this startup status. We look forward to growing and learning alongside you as we unlock the benefits of OI for everyone. Thank you for your support and willingness to join us on this journey.

43

COACHING OI AS A SERVICE

As the business landscape continues to evolve, OI remains a key driver of growth and success. To stay ahead of the competition, businesses must constantly innovate and adapt to changing market conditions, and new technologies that can be used to design, transform and scale radically better ways of working. This is where innovation coaching comes in, specifically OI coaching.

As the founder of ICO, I've seen firsthand the transformative power of innovation in Silicon Valley. Our member content and community site provide a wealth of resources and support for those looking to learn about coaching innovation and deploy OI within their organizations. By joining our community, you'll gain access to experienced innovation coaches and leaders who can help you develop the skills and knowledge you need to succeed as an innovation coach. You'll also have access to a range of free resources and tools such as the digital innovation platform mentioned in this book, that can help you implement OI capabilities within your organization.

At ICO, we believe that innovation is the key to building a better future for all. We're dedicated to helping businesses and individuals alike embrace human-centric innovation especially when innovating with AI and achieving what was previously thought impossible. So why not join us today and start your own innovation coaching journey? Together, we can create a brighter, more innovative, and inclusive future for all.

ABOUT THE AUTHOR

Paul has 30 years experience in leading industrial, technical and social innovation projects, the last 20 using SAP to build integrated cross-functional capabilities. Now with SAP S/4 HANA, he helps clients achieve their strategic objectives by implementing short, medium, and long-term innovation solutions that help to solve the right problems.

After working with Stanford University building an OI digital platform for the School of Medicine 3DQLab, he put design thinking at the forefront of his projects. The Stanford School of Design taught him about using empathy to really help him understand how to build solutions that solve real problems. Now he uses Organizational Innovation to implement SAP S/4, Fiori, SAP Apps, SAP Build, and all the latest SAP Tech, to help solve important and complex challenges.

From his early years transforming supply chains and automating production in factories, overhauling a large retail culture, to building automotive databases for Toyota and many other global businesses, he has always loved the nexus of people, technology, and process, because that's all about creating Organizational Innovation in ways that contribute to the success journey of employees and their organizations.

www.ingramcontent.com/pod-product-compliance
Lightning Source LLC
Chambersburg PA
CBHW031620210526
45464CB00004B/1676